Savor the Taste of the Mediterranean

Explore the Science, Principles, and Irresistible Recipes for a Balanced and Flavorful Lifestyle

Francisca Cornett

Summary

1. *Introduction*
1.1 Overview of the Mediterranean Diet

The Mediterranean Diet is a dietary pattern inspired by the traditional eating habits of countries bordering the Mediterranean Sea. It has gained recognition worldwide for its potential health benefits and has become a popular choice for individuals seeking a balanced and nutritious way of eating.

At its core, the Mediterranean Diet emphasizes the consumption of whole, unprocessed foods that are rich in nutrients and minimizes the intake of processed and refined foods. It is characterized by an abundance of fruits and vegetables, whole grains, legumes, nuts, and healthy fats, such as olive oil. Additionally, moderate consumption of fish, poultry, eggs, and dairy products is included, while red meat and sweets are limited.

One of the key principles of the Mediterranean Diet is the use of olive oil as the primary source of fat. Olive oil is known for its high content of monounsaturated fats, which have been linked to various health benefits, including reduced risk of heart disease. It is used in cooking, dressings, and as a flavor enhancer in many Mediterranean dishes.

Another important aspect of this dietary pattern is the regular consumption of fruits and vegetables. These plant-based foods provide a wide range of vitamins, minerals, and antioxidants that support overall health and protect against chronic diseases. They are typically consumed in their natural form, either raw or cooked, and are a significant source of dietary fiber.

Whole grains, such as whole wheat, oats, and brown rice, are preferred over refined grains like white bread and pasta. These whole grains are rich in fiber and provide sustained energy, promoting a feeling of fullness and aiding in digestion.

The Mediterranean Diet also incorporates a moderate intake of lean proteins, including fish and seafood, which are excellent sources of omega-3 fatty acids. Omega-3s are known for their anti-inflammatory properties and have been associated with heart health and improved cognitive function. Poultry, eggs, and dairy products are consumed in moderation, providing additional sources of protein and essential nutrients.

Herbs and spices play a significant role in Mediterranean cuisine, not only for their flavor but also for their potential health benefits. Common herbs and spices used include basil, oregano, rosemary, garlic, and turmeric, among others. These natural seasonings add depth and complexity to dishes while reducing the need for excessive salt or unhealthy condiments.

In addition to its focus on nutritious foods, the Mediterranean Diet encompasses a holistic lifestyle approach. It emphasizes regular physical activity, such as walking, cycling, or engaging in outdoor activities, as well as fostering a sense of community and social interaction. The Mediterranean culture places importance on enjoying meals with family and friends, savoring the flavors and taking time to appreciate the dining experience.

Numerous scientific studies have linked the Mediterranean Diet to a reduced risk of chronic diseases, including heart disease, type 2 diabetes, and certain types of cancer. It is also associated with improved weight management, cognitive function, and overall longevity.

While the Mediterranean Diet offers a flexible and inclusive approach to eating, it is important to note that there is no one-size-fits-all approach to nutrition. Individual preferences, cultural backgrounds, and health conditions may require adjustments to suit specific needs. Consulting with a healthcare professional or registered dietitian can provide personalized guidance and ensure optimal health outcomes.

Overall, the Mediterranean Diet promotes a balanced and enjoyable way of eating that focuses on whole, nutrient-dense foods, while also encompassing lifestyle factors that contribute to overall well-being. By adopting the principles of the Mediterranean Diet, individuals can nourish their bodies, support their health, and embrace a sustainable approach to nutrition.

1.2 Historical Background

The historical background of the Mediterranean Diet is deeply rooted in the cultures and traditions of the Mediterranean region. It reflects the dietary patterns and practices that have been followed by the inhabitants of countries like Greece, Italy, Spain, and other surrounding nations for centuries.

The origins of the Mediterranean Diet can be traced back to ancient times, with influences from various civilizations that flourished in the region. These civilizations, including the ancient Greeks, Romans, and Egyptians, relied heavily on agriculture, fishing, and trade to sustain their populations.

Historically, the Mediterranean region has been blessed with a favorable climate, fertile soil, and access to the Mediterranean Sea, providing a rich variety of fresh and locally available foods.

The diet developed as a reflection of the available resources and the cultural practices of these societies.

The agricultural practices in the Mediterranean region focused on cultivating a diverse range of crops, including fruits, vegetables, grains, legumes, and olives. The cultivation of grapes and the production of wine also played a significant role in the region's history and cultural practices.

Fish and seafood were abundant in the Mediterranean Sea and were an essential part of the diet. Fishing communities relied on these marine resources for sustenance and trade, contributing to the inclusion of fish in the traditional Mediterranean Diet.

Olive oil, a staple of the Mediterranean Diet, has a long history dating back to ancient civilizations. Olive trees were cultivated and cherished for their valuable fruits, which provided oil for cooking, dressing, and preserving food. Olive oil remains a prominent feature of the Mediterranean Diet, representing the primary source of dietary fat.

The Mediterranean region's history is marked by cultural exchange and trade routes, connecting different societies and introducing new foods and flavors. Phoenician, Arab, and Ottoman influences, among others, have left their mark on the Mediterranean Diet, contributing to its diversity and adaptability.

In the mid-20th century, an American scientist named Ancel Keys brought the Mediterranean Diet to the attention of the world through his studies on cardiovascular health. He observed that populations in the Mediterranean region had lower rates of heart disease compared to those in Western countries, despite a relatively high intake of fat.

Keys' research helped popularize the Mediterranean Diet as a healthy eating pattern. It gained recognition for its potential to promote heart health, weight management, and overall well-being. Since then, numerous studies have reinforced the benefits of the Mediterranean Diet and its association with a reduced risk of chronic diseases.

Today, the Mediterranean Diet has transcended geographical boundaries and has become a global phenomenon. It is embraced by people worldwide as a model for healthy eating and is promoted by health organizations and experts for its potential health benefits.

The historical background of the Mediterranean Diet showcases how the dietary practices of ancient civilizations, coupled with the bountiful resources of the Mediterranean region, have shaped a holistic and healthful way of eating. It is a testament to the wisdom and time-tested traditions of the Mediterranean people, providing valuable insights into the connection between food, culture, and well-being.

1.3 Health Benefits of the Mediterranean Diet

The Mediterranean Diet has gained recognition for its potential health benefits, supported by scientific research and epidemiological studies. This dietary pattern, inspired by the traditional eating habits of Mediterranean countries, has been associated with a variety of positive outcomes for overall well-being.

One of the primary health benefits of the Mediterranean Diet is its potential to promote heart health. Research has consistently shown that adhering to this dietary pattern is associated with a reduced risk of heart disease, including heart attacks, strokes, and high blood pressure. The emphasis on whole, unprocessed foods and the inclusion of healthy fats, such as olive oil and nuts, contributes to its heart-protective effects.

Type 2 diabetes prevention and management is another area where the Mediterranean Diet has demonstrated positive impacts. Studies have found that following this dietary pattern can help improve blood sugar control and insulin sensitivity, reducing the risk of developing type 2 diabetes. The abundance of fiber-rich foods, including fruits, vegetables, and whole grains, along with the moderate consumption of carbohydrates, contributes to its favorable effects on blood sugar regulation.

The Mediterranean Diet has also been associated with weight management and a reduced risk of obesity. The emphasis on nutrient-dense foods, such as fruits, vegetables, and lean proteins, along with the inclusion of healthy fats and portion control, can support a healthy body weight. Additionally, the Mediterranean lifestyle promotes regular physical activity, which further contributes to weight management.

Studies have suggested a potential link between the Mediterranean Diet and improved cognitive function, including a reduced risk of cognitive decline and neurodegenerative diseases, such as Alzheimer's disease. The high intake of fruits, vegetables, and healthy fats, along with the presence of antioxidants and anti-inflammatory compounds in the diet, may play a role in protecting brain health and supporting cognitive function.

The Mediterranean Diet has also been associated with a decreased risk of certain types of cancer. The consumption of a wide variety of plant-based foods, including fruits, vegetables, whole grains, and legumes, provides a rich source of antioxidants, vitamins, minerals, and phytochemicals that have been shown to have potential cancer-protective effects.

Furthermore, the Mediterranean Diet has been linked to longevity and improved overall health outcomes. The combination of a balanced nutrient profile, high intake of plant-based foods, and the inclusion of healthy fats and lean proteins can contribute to overall well-being and a reduced risk of chronic diseases. The Mediterranean lifestyle, with its focus on physical activity, stress reduction, and social connection, further supports a healthy and fulfilling life.

It is important to note that the health benefits of the Mediterranean Diet are not attributed to any single food or nutrient but rather to the overall dietary pattern and lifestyle factors. Additionally, individual variations, genetic factors, and other lifestyle choices can influence the impact of the Mediterranean Diet on health outcomes.

In summary, the Mediterranean Diet has been extensively studied and associated with a range of health benefits, including heart health, diabetes prevention, weight management, cognitive function, cancer prevention, and overall longevity. Emphasizing whole, unprocessed foods, healthy fats, and a balanced nutrient profile, while incorporating physical activity and other lifestyle factors, contributes to the positive impact of the Mediterranean Diet on overall well-being.

2. The Mediterranean Lifestyle
2.1 Cultural Aspects of the Mediterranean Region

The cultural aspects of the Mediterranean region play a significant role in shaping the Mediterranean Diet and lifestyle. The traditions, customs, and social practices of the Mediterranean people contribute to a holistic approach to food, community, and well-being.

Food holds a central place in Mediterranean culture. Meals are not merely a means of nourishment but a time for connection, celebration, and enjoyment. The Mediterranean Diet reflects the importance of communal dining, with family and friends often gathering to share meals together. This cultural practice fosters a sense of belonging and strengthens social bonds.

In the Mediterranean region, meals are typically enjoyed at a leisurely pace, with emphasis on savoring flavors and engaging in conversations. This mindful approach to eating allows individuals to fully appreciate the sensory experience of food, enhancing the satisfaction derived from meals. It also promotes better digestion and overall well-being.

The Mediterranean culture places value on fresh, seasonal, and locally sourced ingredients. Farmers' markets and local produce play a significant role in daily life, where people have access to a wide variety of fruits, vegetables, herbs, and spices. This emphasis on seasonal eating ensures the consumption of diverse nutrients while supporting local agriculture and sustainable food systems.

Hospitality is deeply ingrained in Mediterranean culture. Guests are welcomed with open arms and treated to generous portions of homemade meals. Sharing food is seen as an expression of love, care, and hospitality. The Mediterranean Dict embodies this spirit of generosity and sharing, with dishes often prepared with love and served in abundance.

The Mediterranean region's geography and climate contribute to the availability of fresh produce, seafood, and olive oil, which are key components of the diet. The proximity to the Mediterranean Sea allows for a rich variety of fish and seafood options, which are staples of the Mediterranean Diet. Olive trees thrive in the region's Mediterranean climate, providing a bountiful supply of olive oil—a cornerstone of the diet and a symbol of its cultural heritage.

Culinary traditions are passed down through generations in the Mediterranean. Family recipes, cooking techniques, and flavor combinations are treasured and preserved. Traditional cooking methods, such as slow cooking, grilling, and braising, enhance the flavors and textures of ingredients. The use of herbs, spices, and aromatic ingredients adds depth and complexity to dishes.

In addition to food, physical activity is a fundamental part of the Mediterranean lifestyle. The region's pleasant climate and picturesque landscapes encourage outdoor activities, such as walking, cycling, and gardening. These activities are not only seen as a way to stay physically fit but also as opportunities for social interaction and enjoyment of nature.

Mediterranean culture also embraces a relaxed attitude towards life. Stress management and work-life balance are valued. People prioritize leisure time, taking breaks to enjoy a coffee or engage in conversation with friends. The Mediterranean lifestyle encourages relaxation techniques, such as meditation, napping, or spending time in nature, to promote mental and emotional well-being.

In summary, the cultural aspects of the Mediterranean region encompass the social, culinary, and lifestyle practices that shape the Mediterranean Diet. The focus on communal dining, seasonal and locally sourced ingredients, hospitality, traditional cooking methods, physical activity, and a relaxed approach to life contribute to the holistic and healthful nature of the Mediterranean way of living. These cultural aspects not only nourish the body but also foster connections, enhance well-being, and bring joy to everyday life.

2.2 Physical Activity and Exercise

Physical activity and exercise are integral components of a healthy lifestyle, complementing the dietary patterns of the Mediterranean region. In the context of the Mediterranean Diet, physical activity refers to any form of movement that engages the body's muscles and requires energy expenditure.

The Mediterranean culture encourages a lifestyle that embraces physical activity as a natural part of daily life. This includes activities such as walking, cycling, gardening, and engaging in outdoor pursuits. These activities are often incorporated into everyday routines, promoting a more active lifestyle.

Walking is particularly prominent in Mediterranean communities. It serves as a means of transportation, a way to connect with nature, and a form of exercise. Whether strolling along coastal paths, exploring historical sites, or meandering through vibrant neighborhoods, walking allows individuals to engage in physical activity while immersing themselves in the rich cultural and natural surroundings of the Mediterranean region.

Cycling is another popular form of physical activity in the Mediterranean. With its scenic landscapes and well-developed cycling routes, individuals can enjoy the benefits of cardiovascular exercise while exploring their surroundings. Cycling provides a low-impact workout that enhances cardiovascular health and strengthens leg muscles.

Gardening is deeply rooted in Mediterranean culture, combining physical activity with the joy of cultivating plants and nurturing the land. Tending to a garden involves various movements, such as digging, planting, weeding, and watering, which provide opportunities for moderate-intensity exercise. Gardening promotes flexibility, muscle strength, and mental well-being, as individuals connect with nature and witness the fruits of their labor.

The Mediterranean lifestyle also encompasses recreational activities that embrace the sea, such as swimming, sailing, and paddleboarding. These activities offer a range of physical benefits, including cardiovascular conditioning, improved muscular strength and endurance, and enhanced mental well-being through the calming effect of water.

Engaging in physical activity and exercise is not limited to outdoor pursuits. The Mediterranean culture also embraces indoor activities that promote movement and well-being. These may include dance, yoga, Pilates, and other forms of exercise classes that provide opportunities for strengthening the body, improving flexibility, and reducing stress.

The benefits of physical activity and exercise extend beyond physical health. Regular physical activity has been linked to improved mental well-being, reduced stress levels, increased energy, and enhanced cognitive function. It promotes the release of endorphins, often referred to as "feel-good" hormones, which contribute to a positive mood and overall sense of well-being.

Incorporating physical activity into daily life is not about adhering to rigid exercise routines or intense workouts. It is about finding enjoyable activities that suit individual preferences and abilities. The Mediterranean approach emphasizes the integration of movement into everyday activities, fostering an active lifestyle that is sustainable and enjoyable.

It is important to consult with healthcare professionals or fitness experts to determine appropriate physical activity levels based on individual circumstances, including age, fitness level, and any underlying health conditions.

In summary, physical activity and exercise are fundamental components of the Mediterranean lifestyle. Whether through outdoor activities like walking and cycling, tending to gardens, enjoying water-based pursuits, or participating in indoor exercise classes, the Mediterranean culture encourages individuals to embrace movement and make it an integral part of daily life. Regular physical activity promotes physical and mental well-being, enhances overall health, and complements the balanced dietary patterns of the Mediterranean Diet.

2.3 Stress Management and Relaxation Techniques

Stress management and relaxation techniques are essential components of the Mediterranean lifestyle, contributing to overall well-being and a balanced approach to health. The Mediterranean culture recognizes the importance of maintaining mental and emotional equilibrium in the face of life's challenges.

Stress management involves adopting strategies to cope with stressors and promote a sense of calm and relaxation. The Mediterranean region embraces various approaches to managing stress, which are deeply rooted in cultural traditions and everyday practices.

One of the key aspects of stress management in the Mediterranean culture is fostering a relaxed and leisurely pace of life. Unlike the fast-paced lifestyle prevalent in many Western societies, the Mediterranean way of living encourages individuals to slow down, savor the present moment, and create time for relaxation. This may involve taking breaks during the day, engaging in enjoyable activities, and finding balance between work and personal life.

Nature plays a significant role in stress reduction within the Mediterranean culture. The region's picturesque landscapes, including coastlines, mountains, and countryside, provide opportunities for individuals to connect with nature and experience its calming influence. Whether through walks along the beach, hikes in nature, or simply spending time outdoors, being in natural surroundings is considered therapeutic and helps alleviate stress.

Social connections and community support are also important aspects of stress management in the Mediterranean region. Maintaining strong relationships, spending time with loved ones, and participating in social activities contribute to a sense of belonging and emotional well-being. Engaging in conversations, sharing meals, and participating in communal celebrations are all ways to foster social connections and alleviate stress.

Mindfulness and relaxation techniques are valued in the Mediterranean culture as tools for stress reduction. Practices such as meditation, deep breathing exercises, and yoga are incorporated into daily routines to promote relaxation and mental clarity. These techniques encourage individuals to be fully present in the moment, cultivating awareness of their thoughts, feelings, and physical sensations.

Music, art, and literature are also considered powerful stress-relieving outlets in the Mediterranean culture. Engaging in creative pursuits, such as playing musical instruments, painting, or reading, allows individuals to express themselves, find solace, and disconnect from daily pressures.

Another aspect of stress management in the Mediterranean region is the concept of siesta or afternoon rest. Traditionally, people in Mediterranean countries would take a midday break to rest, nap, or engage in quiet activities. This practice acknowledges the importance of allowing time for rejuvenation and restoring energy levels.

It is important to note that stress management and relaxation techniques are highly individualized, and what works for one person may not work for another. Exploring and finding personal strategies that resonate with an individual's preferences and needs is key to effective stress management.

In summary, stress management and relaxation techniques are integral to the Mediterranean lifestyle. Embracing a relaxed pace of life, connecting with nature, fostering social connections, practicing mindfulness, engaging in creative pursuits, and prioritizing rest are all ways in which the Mediterranean culture promotes stress reduction and overall well-being. By incorporating these practices into daily life, individuals can cultivate a greater sense of balance, resilience, and emotional well-being.

3. Key Components of the Mediterranean Diet

3.1 Fruits and Vegetables

Fruits and vegetables form a foundational component of the Mediterranean Diet, representing a rich and diverse array of plant-based foods. They are cherished for their nutritional value, flavors, and vibrant colors, and are considered essential for maintaining overall health and well-being.

The Mediterranean culture celebrates the abundance of fruits and vegetables available in the region. These plant-based foods are a cornerstone of meals, consumed in various forms—raw, cooked, or incorporated into traditional dishes. They are often sourced from local markets and reflect the seasonal offerings of the land.

Fruits and vegetables provide a wide range of vitamins, minerals, antioxidants, and dietary fiber. They are nature's nutritional powerhouses, offering essential nutrients that support vital bodily functions and help protect against chronic diseases. The Mediterranean Diet encourages the consumption of a variety of fruits and vegetables, as each type offers a unique nutrient profile and health benefits.

The vibrant colors of fruits and vegetables reflect the presence of different phytochemicals, which are natural compounds with potential health-promoting properties. These phytochemicals act as antioxidants, protecting the body against oxidative stress and inflammation. The Mediterranean Diet's emphasis on a colorful assortment of fruits and vegetables ensures a broad spectrum of these beneficial compounds.

Leafy green vegetables, such as spinach, kale, and Swiss chard, are particularly valued in the Mediterranean Diet. They are rich in vitamins A, C, and K, as well as minerals like iron and calcium. Leafy greens are often incorporated into salads, stews, or used as a side dish, providing a nutritious boost to meals.

Tomatoes, peppers, eggplants, and zucchinis are popular vegetables in Mediterranean cuisine. They are versatile ingredients, appearing in various dishes, including salads, stews, and grilled or roasted preparations. These vegetables are sources of vitamins, minerals, and antioxidants that contribute to overall health and provide a burst of flavor to Mediterranean recipes.

Fruits, such as oranges, lemons, grapes, figs, and pomegranates, are abundant in the Mediterranean region. They offer a natural sweetness and refreshing taste, making them a delightful addition to meals and desserts. Fruits are not only rich in vitamins, minerals, and antioxidants but also provide dietary fiber, which supports digestive health and helps maintain healthy blood sugar levels.

The Mediterranean culture encourages the consumption of whole, unprocessed fruits and vegetables rather than relying on juices or highly processed forms. This ensures that individuals benefit from the full range of nutrients and dietary fiber that whole foods provide.

In the Mediterranean Diet, fruits and vegetables are celebrated not only for their nutritional value but also for their role in enhancing the sensory experience of eating. Their inclusion in meals contributes to the visual appeal, flavors, and textures that make Mediterranean dishes enticing and enjoyable.

While fruits and vegetables are essential components of the Mediterranean Diet, it is important to note that the overall dietary pattern, which includes other food groups and lifestyle factors, contributes to the health benefits observed. The Mediterranean Diet emphasizes a holistic approach to nutrition, with the inclusion of fruits and vegetables being one of its key pillars.

In summary, fruits and vegetables are highly regarded in Mediterranean culture for their nutritional value, flavors, and visual appeal. The Mediterranean Diet emphasizes the consumption of a variety of fruits and vegetables, providing an array of vitamins, minerals, antioxidants, and dietary fiber. Their incorporation into meals adds vibrancy and contributes to the overall health and well-being associated with the Mediterranean way of eating.

3.2 Whole Grains

Whole grains play a significant role in the Mediterranean Diet, serving as a source of nourishment and a key component of balanced meals. Whole grains are grains that have not undergone extensive processing, preserving their natural nutritional composition and fiber content.

In the Mediterranean region, whole grains have been consumed for centuries and are deeply ingrained in cultural traditions. They provide sustenance, energy, and contribute to the overall dietary diversity and balance.

Whole grains encompass a variety of options, including wheat, barley, oats, rice, corn, and rye, among others. These grains are typically consumed in their intact form or minimally processed, preserving the bran, germ, and endosperm—the three main components that contain essential nutrients.

The consumption of whole grains offers several nutritional benefits. They are a rich source of dietary fiber, which supports digestive health, aids in maintaining healthy blood sugar levels, and promotes a feeling of fullness. The fiber content in whole grains helps regulate bowel movements and supports a healthy gut microbiome.

Whole grains also provide important vitamins, minerals, and antioxidants. They contain B vitamins, such as thiamine, riboflavin, and niacin, which are essential for energy production and metabolism. Minerals like magnesium, selenium, and zinc are also present in whole grains, contributing to various bodily functions and overall well-being.

In the Mediterranean Diet, whole grains are consumed as part of balanced meals. They are often used as a base for traditional dishes, such as pilafs, couscous, or risottos. Whole grain bread, pasta, and cereals are common staples in the Mediterranean region.

The inclusion of whole grains in the Mediterranean Diet helps promote sustained energy levels and supports overall health. The complex carbohydrates found in whole grains are broken down slowly by the body, providing a steady release of energy and helping individuals feel satisfied and satiated.

The Mediterranean culture places importance on the quality and preparation of whole grains. Traditional methods of cooking and processing, such as soaking or fermenting, are often employed to enhance their digestibility and nutrient availability. These practices are rooted in the wisdom of generations and contribute to the overall enjoyment and health benefits of consuming whole grains.

While whole grains are a valuable component of the Mediterranean Diet, it is important to consider individual needs and preferences. Some individuals may have dietary restrictions or sensitivities that require modifications or alternative grain options. Consulting with healthcare professionals or registered dietitians can provide personalized guidance and ensure optimal nutrition.

In summary, whole grains form an integral part of the Mediterranean Diet, contributing to the dietary diversity and nutritional balance of meals. With their fiber, vitamins, minerals, and natural composition, whole grains provide sustained energy, support digestive health, and offer a range of health benefits. The Mediterranean culture recognizes the value of whole grains and incorporates them into traditional dishes, embodying the holistic and nourishing approach to eating.

3.3 Healthy Fats and Oils

Healthy fats and oils are fundamental components of the Mediterranean Diet, providing essential nutrients and contributing to overall health and well-being. In the Mediterranean region, the use of specific fats and oils has been a longstanding tradition, deeply rooted in cultural practices and culinary traditions.

The Mediterranean Diet promotes the consumption of healthy fats, while minimizing the intake of unhealthy saturated and trans fats. Healthy fats play important roles in the body, supporting various bodily functions and providing a source of energy.

One of the key sources of healthy fats in the Mediterranean Diet is olive oil. Olive oil is derived from the pressing of olives and is a staple in Mediterranean cuisine. It is a rich source of monounsaturated fats, particularly oleic acid, which is associated with numerous health benefits. Monounsaturated fats have been shown to support heart health, reduce inflammation, and improve cholesterol levels.

Olive oil is used in various culinary applications, such as cooking, salad dressings, and as a flavor enhancer in many Mediterranean dishes. Its distinct flavor and aroma add depth and richness to meals, enhancing the sensory experience of eating.

In addition to olive oil, other sources of healthy fats in the Mediterranean Diet include avocados, nuts, and seeds. These foods provide a combination of monounsaturated and polyunsaturated fats, including omega-3 and omega-6 fatty acids.

Avocados are known for their creamy texture and high monounsaturated fat content. They are a versatile ingredient, used in salads, spreads, or as a topping for various dishes. Nuts and seeds, such as almonds, walnuts, flaxseeds, and chia seeds, are nutrient-dense and offer a range of healthy fats, along with essential vitamins, minerals, and fiber. They can be enjoyed as a snack, incorporated into meals, or used as toppings for salads and yogurt.

Fish and seafood are also significant sources of healthy fats in the Mediterranean Diet. Fatty fish, such as salmon, mackerel, sardines, and trout, are rich in omega-3 fatty acids, particularly eicosapentaenoic acid (EPA) and docosahexaenoic acid (DHA). Omega-3 fatty acids are known for their anti-inflammatory properties and have been associated with various health benefits, including heart health, brain function, and reduced risk of chronic diseases.

The Mediterranean culture embraces the use of healthy fats and oils in moderation, understanding that they contribute to both the taste and nutritional value of meals. The emphasis is on selecting high-quality fats and oils, minimizing the use of processed or hydrogenated fats, and incorporating a variety of sources to ensure a balanced intake of different types of healthy fats.

It is important to note that while healthy fats are beneficial, they are also calorie-dense, so portion control is necessary to maintain a healthy energy balance. It is recommended to consume fats and oils in moderation, as part of a well-balanced diet that includes a variety of other nutrient-dense foods.

In summary, healthy fats and oils are integral components of the Mediterranean Diet, providing essential nutrients and contributing to overall health and well-being. Olive oil, avocados, nuts, seeds, and fatty fish are among the sources of healthy fats in this dietary pattern. These fats offer numerous health benefits, including support for heart health, inflammation reduction, and optimal brain function. The Mediterranean culture values the use of healthy fats in moderation, enhancing the culinary experience while promoting a balanced and nourishing way of eating.

3.4 Legumes and Nuts

Legumes and nuts are essential components of the Mediterranean Diet, providing a wealth of nutrients, plant-based protein, and a variety of flavors and textures. In Mediterranean cuisine, legumes and nuts have long been celebrated for their versatility, taste, and health benefits.

Legumes, which include beans, lentils, chickpeas, and peas, are highly regarded in the Mediterranean region. They are an excellent source of plant-based protein, dietary fiber, vitamins, minerals, and antioxidants. Legumes offer a range of flavors and textures, making them suitable for a wide variety of dishes.

Beans, such as kidney beans, black beans, and cannellini beans, are commonly used in Mediterranean cuisine. They are rich in protein, fiber, and various nutrients, including folate, iron, and magnesium. Beans are often incorporated into stews, soups, salads, and side dishes, providing both sustenance and nutritional value.

Lentils are another legume that holds a special place in Mediterranean cooking. They come in various colors, including green, brown, and red, and offer distinct flavors and textures. Lentils are a great source of plant-based protein, dietary fiber, and minerals like iron and folate. They can be used in a variety of Mediterranean dishes, from salads to hearty soups and stews.

Chickpeas, or garbanzo beans, are a beloved legume in Mediterranean cuisine. They are versatile and commonly used in dishes like hummus, falafel, and stews. Chickpeas are rich in protein, fiber, and essential nutrients such as folate and manganese. They provide a hearty and nutritious addition to meals.

Peas, both green and yellow, are popular legumes in the Mediterranean region. They are often used in soups, stews, and risottos, adding a burst of sweetness and vibrant color to dishes. Peas offer dietary fiber, vitamins, and minerals, contributing to the nutritional value of meals.

Nuts, such as almonds, walnuts, pistachios, and hazelnuts, are highly valued in Mediterranean culture. They are nutrient-dense and provide a rich source of healthy fats, protein, dietary fiber, vitamins, minerals, and antioxidants. Nuts are enjoyed as snacks, added to salads, incorporated into baked goods, or used as toppings for various dishes.

Almonds are a staple in the Mediterranean Diet, offering a delicate and slightly sweet flavor. They are rich in vitamin E, magnesium, and monounsaturated fats, which are associated with heart health. Walnuts are known for their distinct flavor and shape, and they provide omega-3 fatty acids, which have been linked to numerous health benefits. Pistachios and hazelnuts are also treasured for their unique flavors and nutritional profiles, contributing to a diverse range of culinary creations.

The consumption of legumes and nuts in the Mediterranean Diet contributes to overall health and well-being. Legumes offer plant-based protein, dietary fiber, and a variety of nutrients, while nuts provide healthy fats, protein, and essential micronutrients. Their inclusion in meals enhances nutritional diversity, adds texture and flavor, and promotes satiety.

The Mediterranean culture embraces legumes and nuts for their culinary versatility and health benefits. These plant-based foods reflect the region's emphasis on balanced nutrition, offering a satisfying and nutritious way to incorporate plant-based protein and healthy fats into the diet.

In summary, legumes and nuts are integral components of the Mediterranean Diet, providing plant-based protein, dietary fiber, healthy fats, and an array of essential nutrients. The Mediterranean region's appreciation for these ingredients is reflected in their versatile use in various dishes, contributing to the nutritional richness and culinary diversity of Mediterranean cuisine.

3.5 Fish and Seafood

Fish and seafood play a prominent role in the Mediterranean Diet, offering a rich source of protein, essential nutrients, and a unique culinary experience. The Mediterranean region, with its proximity to the sea, has a long-standing tradition of incorporating fish and seafood into its cuisine.

Fish, such as salmon, mackerel, sardines, tuna, and cod, are highly valued in the Mediterranean Diet. They are not only delicious but also provide an excellent source of lean protein and important nutrients like omega-3 fatty acids, vitamins, and minerals. Omega-3 fatty acids, particularly eicosapentaenoic acid (EPA) and docosahexaenoic acid (DHA), have been associated with numerous health benefits, including cardiovascular health and brain function.

The consumption of fish in the Mediterranean region extends beyond its nutritional value. Fishing has been an integral part of Mediterranean culture and history, with fishing communities relying on the sea as a source of sustenance and livelihood. The appreciation for fresh, locally caught fish is deeply ingrained in Mediterranean culinary traditions.

Seafood, which encompasses a wide variety of shellfish and mollusks, is also prized in Mediterranean cuisine. Shrimp, mussels, clams, squid, octopus, and oysters are among the popular choices. Seafood offers a rich source of protein, vitamins, minerals, and antioxidants. Each type of seafood has its own unique taste and texture, contributing to the diverse flavors and culinary experiences of the Mediterranean Diet.

The preparation of fish and seafood in the Mediterranean Diet often involves simple and flavorful techniques. Grilling, baking, poaching, or steaming are popular methods that help preserve the natural flavors and textures of the seafood. The Mediterranean culture values the quality and freshness of ingredients, allowing the natural taste of fish and seafood to shine through.

Fish and seafood are typically served with a variety of accompanying ingredients, such as fresh herbs, olive oil, lemon, garlic, and spices. These additions enhance the flavors of the seafood and provide a delightful sensory experience.

The inclusion of fish and seafood in the Mediterranean Diet provides not only nutritional benefits but also supports sustainable food practices. The emphasis on locally caught, seasonal, and responsibly sourced seafood helps protect marine ecosystems and ensures the long-term availability of these resources.

The Mediterranean culture recognizes the connection between food and community, and fish and seafood are often enjoyed in a social setting. Sharing a meal of fresh fish or seafood with family and friends fosters a sense of togetherness and celebrates the culinary heritage of the region.

It is important to consider individual preferences, dietary restrictions, and sustainability factors when consuming fish and seafood. Some individuals may have allergies or dietary restrictions that limit their intake of certain types of seafood. Consulting with healthcare professionals or local seafood guides can provide guidance on choosing sustainable and appropriate options based on individual circumstances.

In summary, fish and seafood are prized components of the Mediterranean Diet, providing a source of lean protein, essential nutrients, and unique flavors. The Mediterranean culture's connection to the sea and its emphasis on fresh, locally caught ingredients contribute to the appreciation and enjoyment of fish and seafood. Incorporating these ocean treasures into the diet adds nutritional diversity and supports sustainable food practices.

3.6 Poultry and Eggs

Poultry and eggs are components of the Mediterranean Diet, offering a versatile source of protein and a variety of culinary possibilities. While the Mediterranean Diet primarily focuses on plant-based foods, poultry and eggs are included in moderation, providing essential nutrients and contributing to the overall nutritional balance of the diet.

Poultry, such as chicken and turkey, is valued for its lean protein content. It serves as an alternative to red meat and offers a lighter option in the Mediterranean Diet. Poultry is versatile and can be prepared in various ways, including grilling, baking, roasting, or sautéing. The Mediterranean culture often incorporates herbs, spices, and aromatics to enhance the flavors of poultry dishes.

Eggs are a highly nutritious food and a common ingredient in Mediterranean cooking. They are a rich source of high-quality protein, essential vitamins, and minerals. Eggs are used in a wide range of preparations, including omelets, frittatas, quiches, and baked goods. They contribute to the richness and texture of dishes while providing valuable nutrients.

In the Mediterranean Diet, the consumption of poultry and eggs is often balanced with the abundance of plant-based foods. The emphasis is on lean cuts of poultry and moderate portions to maintain a well-rounded and balanced diet.

The Mediterranean culture values the quality and sourcing of poultry and eggs. Whenever possible, choosing free-range, organic, or pasture-raised poultry and eggs is encouraged, as these options align with sustainable and animal welfare considerations.

It is important to note that individual preferences, dietary needs, and cultural practices may influence the inclusion of poultry and eggs in the Mediterranean Diet. Some individuals may choose to incorporate poultry and eggs more frequently, while others may limit or exclude them based on personal choices or dietary restrictions.

In summary, poultry and eggs are part of the Mediterranean Diet, offering a valuable source of lean protein, essential nutrients, and culinary diversity. Poultry provides a lighter alternative to red meat, while eggs contribute to the nutritional richness and versatility of Mediterranean cuisine. Their inclusion, in moderation, adds protein variety and can be adapted to individual preferences and dietary needs.

3.7 Dairy Products

Dairy products are a part of the Mediterranean Diet, providing a source of essential nutrients and contributing to the culinary diversity of the region. While the Mediterranean Diet primarily emphasizes plant-based foods, dairy products have their place in moderation, adding flavor, texture, and nutritional value to meals.

Milk and its derivatives, such as yogurt and cheese, are commonly consumed dairy products in the Mediterranean region. These products offer a rich source of protein, calcium, vitamins, and minerals that support various bodily functions.

Milk, whether cow's milk or other animal milk like goat or sheep milk, is a versatile ingredient used in cooking and baking, as well as a beverage on its own. It provides a source of protein, calcium, vitamin D, and other essential nutrients. Milk is often used as a base for traditional Mediterranean desserts, hot beverages like cappuccino, or in cooking dishes like creamy sauces and soups.

Yogurt is a fermented dairy product that holds a special place in Mediterranean cuisine. It is created by fermenting milk with live bacteria cultures, resulting in a creamy texture and tangy flavor. Yogurt is prized for its probiotic properties, which promote gut health and digestion. It is consumed on its own, incorporated into savory dips and sauces, or used as a topping for fruits and desserts. Greek yogurt, with its thicker consistency, is particularly popular in the Mediterranean region.

Cheese is another dairy product widely consumed in the Mediterranean Diet. There is a wide variety of cheeses available, each offering unique flavors, textures, and culinary uses. Feta, halloumi, ricotta, and Parmesan are examples of cheeses commonly used in Mediterranean cuisine. Cheese provides a source of protein, calcium, and other essential nutrients. It is used in salads, pasta dishes, sandwiches, and as a garnish for various Mediterranean recipes.

The consumption of dairy products in the Mediterranean Diet is often balanced with other food groups to maintain a well-rounded diet. The Mediterranean culture values the quality and sourcing of dairy products. When possible, choosing organic or locally produced dairy products is encouraged, as it supports sustainable and responsible food practices.

It is important to consider individual preferences, dietary needs, and cultural practices when incorporating dairy products into the Mediterranean Diet. Some individuals may have lactose intolerance or other sensitivities, which may require the use of lactose-free or plant-based alternatives.

In summary, dairy products are a part of the Mediterranean Diet, offering a source of protein, calcium, and other essential nutrients. Milk, yogurt, and cheese contribute to the culinary diversity of Mediterranean cuisine, providing flavor, texture, and nutritional value to meals. Their consumption, in moderation, complements the plant-based focus of the diet and can be adapted to individual preferences and dietary needs.

3.8 Herbs and Spices

Herbs and spices are integral elements of Mediterranean cuisine, adding depth, flavor, and aroma to dishes. The Mediterranean region is known for its rich culinary heritage, which embraces the use of various herbs and spices to enhance the sensory experience of food.

Herbs are derived from the leaves of plants and are often used fresh or dried to impart distinctive flavors to meals. Some commonly used herbs in Mediterranean cooking include basil, oregano, rosemary, thyme, parsley, and mint. Each herb offers its own unique flavor profile, ranging from earthy and aromatic to fresh and citrusy. Herbs are often added during cooking or used as garnishes, enhancing the taste and visual appeal of dishes.

Spices, on the other hand, are derived from the seeds, bark, roots, or fruits of plants. They provide intense flavors and are used in smaller quantities compared to herbs. Spices commonly used in Mediterranean cuisine include cinnamon, cumin, paprika, turmeric, coriander, and cloves. These spices bring warmth, complexity, and depth to dishes, often used in spice blends or individually to create distinct flavor profiles.

The Mediterranean culture celebrates the art of combining herbs and spices to create harmonious flavor combinations. The careful balance of these ingredients contributes to the unique taste and character of Mediterranean dishes.

Herbs and spices not only enhance the flavors of food but also offer potential health benefits. Many herbs and spices contain bioactive compounds that have been associated with antioxidant, anti-inflammatory, and antimicrobial properties. For example, turmeric contains curcumin, which has been studied for its potential health benefits, while cinnamon may help regulate blood sugar levels.

In Mediterranean cuisine, herbs and spices are used to elevate a wide range of dishes. From pasta sauces and stews to grilled meats and seafood, these ingredients play a crucial role in creating the vibrant and diverse flavors that are characteristic of the Mediterranean Diet.

The use of herbs and spices in the Mediterranean region reflects the availability of local, fresh ingredients. Many households cultivate their own herb gardens, ensuring a ready supply of aromatic herbs. The Mediterranean culture values the use of high-quality, authentic herbs and spices, enhancing the overall culinary experience.

It is important to note that individual preferences, cultural practices, and dietary considerations may influence the selection and use of herbs and spices. Some individuals may have allergies or sensitivities to certain herbs or spices, while others may prefer milder or more intense flavors. Exploring different combinations and adapting recipes to personal tastes is part of the culinary adventure offered by herbs and spices.

In summary, herbs and spices are fundamental to Mediterranean cuisine, enriching dishes with flavors, aromas, and potential health benefits. The Mediterranean culture embraces the use of herbs and spices to create vibrant and diverse flavors, elevating the sensory experience of meals. Whether in fresh or dried form, these ingredients contribute to the culinary heritage and uniqueness of the Mediterranean Diet.

3.9 Red Wine in Moderation

Red wine, when consumed in moderation, is a component of the Mediterranean Diet that is often celebrated for its cultural and potential health benefits. In the Mediterranean region, red wine has been enjoyed for centuries, forming an integral part of social gatherings and meals.

Moderate consumption of red wine refers to drinking in a responsible manner, typically defined as one glass per day for women and up to two glasses per day for men. This moderate approach acknowledges that excessive alcohol consumption can have adverse effects on health and well-being.

Red wine is made from the fermentation of dark-colored grapes, and it offers a unique combination of flavors, aromas, and compounds. It contains alcohol, as well as various bioactive substances, including polyphenols and antioxidants. These compounds, such as resveratrol and flavonoids, have attracted scientific interest due to their potential health benefits.

The potential health benefits associated with red wine are thought to be attributed to these bioactive compounds. Resveratrol, in particular, has been studied for its antioxidant and anti-inflammatory properties, which may contribute to heart health and reduced risk of certain diseases. Flavonoids, on the other hand, have been linked to improved blood vessel function and reduced oxidative stress.

In the Mediterranean culture, red wine is often consumed as part of meals, complementing the flavors of food and enhancing the overall dining experience. It is savored slowly, allowing individuals to appreciate its complexities and enjoy the social aspect of sharing a glass with others.

It is important to note that the potential health benefits of red wine should not overshadow the importance of overall healthy lifestyle habits. Red wine is just one component of the Mediterranean Diet, which emphasizes a balanced approach to eating, including a variety of plant-based foods, lean proteins, and healthy fats, as well as regular physical activity and social connections.

Individuals should also be mindful of their own health conditions, medication use, and personal circumstances when considering the consumption of red wine. For some individuals, the risks associated with alcohol consumption may outweigh the potential benefits. It is always recommended to consult with healthcare professionals for personalized advice.

In summary, red wine, when consumed in moderation, is a cherished component of the Mediterranean Diet. It adds to the culinary experience and social enjoyment of meals. Red wine contains bioactive compounds, such as resveratrol and flavonoids, which have been associated with potential health benefits. However, it is important to remember that moderation is key, and overall healthy lifestyle habits are crucial for promoting well-being.

4. Planning and Implementing the Mediterranean Diet

4.1 Setting Goals and Assessing Current Eating Habits

Setting goals and assessing current eating habits are important steps in making positive changes to one's diet and overall health. These processes involve self-reflection, planning, and developing a clear understanding of one's current dietary patterns and desired outcomes.

Setting goals involves identifying specific targets or objectives that one aims to achieve. These goals can be related to various aspects of eating habits, such as increasing fruit and vegetable intake, reducing added sugar consumption, or improving portion control. The goals should be realistic, achievable, and tailored to individual preferences and circumstances.

Assessing current eating habits involves taking a comprehensive look at one's dietary patterns, food choices, portion sizes, meal frequency, and overall nutritional balance. This process requires self-awareness and honest reflection. It may involve keeping a food diary, noting eating patterns, and paying attention to emotional or environmental triggers that influence food choices.

By assessing current eating habits, individuals can identify areas of improvement and gain insight into the factors that contribute to unhealthy eating patterns. This information serves as a foundation for setting goals that align with personal needs and priorities.

It is important to approach goal setting and assessment without judgment or criticism. The purpose is to foster a positive and constructive mindset, focusing on making gradual, sustainable changes rather than pursuing extreme or restrictive measures. Each person's journey is unique, and the emphasis should be on progress rather than perfection.

Goal setting and assessment are ongoing processes that may require adjustments and refinements along the way. Regular self-reflection and evaluation can help track progress, identify barriers or challenges, and make necessary adaptations to ensure continued growth and improvement.

These practices are often best undertaken with the guidance of healthcare professionals or registered dietitians who can provide personalized recommendations and support. They can help individuals set realistic goals, offer insights into optimal nutrition, and provide strategies for overcoming obstacles.

In summary, setting goals and assessing current eating habits are crucial steps in making positive changes to one's diet and overall health. By setting realistic goals and honestly evaluating current dietary patterns, individuals can develop a clear understanding of their needs, preferences, and areas for improvement. These processes foster self-awareness, provide a foundation for meaningful change, and contribute to a sustainable and balanced approach to healthy eating.

4.2 Grocery Shopping and Meal Planning

Grocery shopping and meal planning are essential aspects of maintaining a healthy and well-balanced diet. These practices involve thoughtful consideration, preparation, and organization to ensure that the right foods are available and meals can be prepared efficiently.

Grocery shopping is the process of selecting and purchasing food items from stores or markets. It involves making choices based on personal preferences, dietary needs, and planned meals. When grocery shopping, individuals typically consider factors such as nutritional content, freshness, quality, and affordability.

Meal planning entails determining in advance what meals will be prepared and consumed during a certain period of time. It involves selecting recipes, considering dietary goals, and creating a shopping list of necessary ingredients. Meal planning can be done on a daily, weekly, or monthly basis, depending on individual preferences and circumstances.

Both grocery shopping and meal planning are interconnected and complement each other. By engaging in meal planning, individuals can make informed choices when grocery shopping, ensuring that they have the necessary ingredients on hand to prepare nutritious meals. This approach also helps minimize food waste and encourages healthier eating habits.

Effective grocery shopping and meal planning involve considering a variety of food groups, such as fruits, vegetables, whole grains, lean proteins, and healthy fats. It is important to aim for a diverse range of ingredients that provide essential nutrients and support overall health and well-being.

When grocery shopping, individuals may also consider factors such as seasonality, local produce availability, and sustainable sourcing practices. These considerations align with the principles of the Mediterranean Diet, which emphasize fresh, whole foods and support environmentally conscious food choices.

Meal planning can be approached flexibly to accommodate individual preferences and lifestyles. Some individuals may prefer detailed planning, while others may opt for a more flexible framework that allows for improvisation and creativity in the kitchen. The goal is to have a general idea of the meals that will be prepared, ensuring that a variety of nutritious options are available.

Both grocery shopping and meal planning can be tailored to individual needs, such as dietary restrictions, cultural preferences, or specific health goals. Seeking guidance from healthcare professionals or registered dietitians can provide personalized recommendations and support in creating a meal plan that suits individual circumstances.

In summary, grocery shopping and meal planning are important practices that support healthy eating habits. By carefully selecting and purchasing nutritious foods, and by planning meals in advance, individuals can ensure that they have the necessary ingredients and structure in place to prepare balanced and nourishing meals. These practices contribute to a well-rounded approach to nutrition and can be adapted to suit individual preferences and dietary goals.

4.3 Cooking Techniques and Recipes

Cooking techniques and recipes are integral components of preparing delicious and nutritious meals. They provide the framework and guidance for transforming ingredients into flavorful dishes that satisfy both the palate and nutritional needs.

Cooking techniques refer to the methods and processes used to prepare food. They encompass a wide range of approaches, including baking, grilling, sautéing, steaming, boiling, roasting, and simmering, among others. Each cooking technique offers unique results in terms of flavors, textures, and nutritional profiles.

Recipes serve as a blueprint for preparing specific dishes, outlining the ingredients and step-by-step instructions. They provide guidance on ingredient quantities, cooking times, and the combination of flavors and techniques to achieve desired results.

Recipes can range from simple and quick meals to elaborate and multi-course creations.

Different cooking techniques can be used to highlight the natural flavors and textures of ingredients. For example, grilling vegetables enhances their smoky and charred notes, while steaming preserves their crispness and vibrant colors. Roasting meats at a high temperature can create a golden crust, while simmering stews and soups slowly develops deep flavors.

Recipes serve as a source of inspiration and creativity in the kitchen. They often reflect cultural traditions, personal preferences, and regional influences. Recipes can be modified and adapted to suit individual tastes, dietary restrictions, or ingredient availability. They allow individuals to explore new flavors, experiment with ingredients, and develop their culinary skills.

Cooking techniques and recipes play an essential role in the Mediterranean Diet, which emphasizes the use of fresh, whole ingredients and a variety of flavors. Mediterranean cooking techniques include grilling seafood, roasting vegetables, and simmering stews. Recipes range from classic dishes like Greek salad or ratatouille to regional specialties such as paella or couscous.

The Mediterranean culture values the art of cooking and the sharing of meals. Cooking techniques and recipes serve as a means of preserving cultural heritage and promoting social connections. Traditional recipes are passed down through generations, capturing the essence of a region's culinary identity.

Exploring different cooking techniques and recipes allows individuals to broaden their culinary horizons and discover new flavors. It encourages creativity, fosters a sense of accomplishment, and promotes a healthier relationship with food by encouraging the use of fresh ingredients and minimizing reliance on processed foods.

It is important to approach cooking techniques and recipes with a mindset of enjoyment and exploration. Experimenting with ingredients, adjusting flavors, and adapting recipes to personal preferences are all part of the culinary journey. Learning from experience and developing one's cooking skills can lead to a greater appreciation for food and the satisfaction of creating nourishing meals.

In summary, cooking techniques and recipes are fundamental in preparing delicious and nutritious meals. Cooking techniques encompass a range of methods used to transform ingredients, while recipes provide guidance and inspiration for creating specific dishes. They promote creativity, cultural preservation, and a healthier approach to food. Exploring different techniques and recipes can lead to culinary adventures and the development of cooking skills that enhance the enjoyment and satisfaction of meals.

4.4 Portion Control and Mindful Eating

Portion control and mindful eating are practices that promote a balanced and healthy approach to consuming food. They involve paying attention to serving sizes, listening to the body's hunger and fullness cues, and cultivating a mindful awareness of the eating experience.

Portion control refers to being mindful of the quantity of food consumed. It involves understanding appropriate portion sizes and moderating the amount of food on the plate. By practicing portion control, individuals can avoid overeating and maintain a healthy energy balance.

Mindful eating, on the other hand, focuses on the quality of the eating experience. It involves being fully present and engaged during meals, savoring the flavors, textures, and aromas of food. Mindful eating encourages a non-judgmental attitude towards food and fosters a deeper connection with the body's hunger and satiety signals.

Both portion control and mindful eating contribute to a balanced approach to nutrition. By being aware of portion sizes, individuals can ensure that they are consuming appropriate amounts of food for their energy needs. This can help prevent excessive calorie intake and support weight management.

Mindful eating promotes a greater appreciation for food, fostering a healthier relationship with eating. It encourages individuals to slow down, savor each bite, and tune in to their body's signals of hunger and fullness. This practice can help prevent overeating, promote better digestion, and enhance the enjoyment of meals.

Portion control and mindful eating are particularly relevant in the context of the Mediterranean Diet. This dietary pattern emphasizes the quality of food, the pleasure of eating, and the cultural aspects of meals. By practicing portion control and mindful eating within the context of the Mediterranean Diet, individuals can fully experience the flavors and nutritional benefits of the diverse array of foods in this eating pattern.

It is important to approach portion control and mindful eating without strict rules or judgment. Each individual's needs and preferences may vary, and it is essential to respect personal hunger and satiety cues. Portion control and mindful eating should be practiced in a way that supports overall well-being and nourishment rather than creating stress or deprivation.

Developing portion control and mindful eating habits takes time and practice. It may involve paying attention to hunger and fullness cues, using smaller plates or bowls, taking time to chew food thoroughly, and minimizing distractions during meals. Incorporating these practices gradually and finding what works best for each individual can lead to a more balanced and enjoyable approach to eating.

In summary, portion control and mindful eating are practices that promote a balanced and healthy relationship with food. Portion control involves being mindful of serving sizes, while mindful eating cultivates a present and attentive attitude towards the eating experience. By practicing portion control and mindful eating, individuals can maintain a healthy energy balance, prevent overeating, and fully appreciate the flavors and nourishment of meals.

4.5 Eating Out and Social Situations

Eating out and social situations present unique challenges and opportunities when it comes to maintaining a healthy and balanced diet. These occasions often involve dining at restaurants, attending social gatherings, or sharing meals with friends and family. Navigating these situations requires mindful decision-making and adapting to different food environments.

When eating out, individuals may encounter a wide range of food options, from indulgent dishes to healthier choices. It can be helpful to approach dining out with a mindful mindset, considering factors such as portion sizes, cooking methods, and ingredient quality. Making conscious choices and prioritizing nutrient-dense options can contribute to a balanced meal.

In social situations, there may be cultural or social expectations surrounding food choices and eating habits. It is important to find a balance between honoring traditions and personal dietary goals. Communication and planning ahead can be useful in ensuring that there are suitable options available or making adjustments to accommodate personal preferences.

When faced with a variety of food choices, mindful decision-making involves tuning in to personal hunger and satiety cues, making choices that align with one's dietary needs and goals, and finding satisfaction in the overall eating experience. It is also important to be kind to oneself and practice self-compassion, acknowledging that occasional indulgences or deviations from routine are part of a balanced approach to eating.

In social situations, it can be beneficial to focus on the social connections and enjoyment of the company, rather than solely on the food. Engaging in meaningful conversations, being present, and savoring the experience can enhance the overall satisfaction of the gathering.

Adapting to different food environments requires flexibility and open-mindedness. It may involve exploring new flavors, trying unfamiliar dishes, or seeking out healthier alternatives when possible. It can also involve finding ways to balance indulgences with mindful choices, such as sharing desserts or selecting smaller portions.

When faced with limited healthy options or unfamiliar cuisines, it can be helpful to approach the situation with curiosity and a willingness to experiment. Exploring different foods and flavors can be an opportunity to broaden culinary horizons and discover new favorites.

It is important to remember that eating out and social situations are part of a larger lifestyle and dietary pattern. Consistency and balance in overall eating habits are key, and occasional deviations or special occasions should be viewed in the context of the bigger picture.

By approaching eating out and social situations with mindfulness, awareness, and adaptability, individuals can navigate these situations in a way that supports their overall health and well-being. Balancing enjoyment, connection, and personal dietary goals contributes to a positive and sustainable approach to eating in a variety of social contexts.

In summary, eating out and social situations present unique challenges and opportunities when it comes to maintaining a healthy and balanced diet. Mindful decision-making, adapting to different food environments, and finding a balance between personal preferences and social expectations are essential in these situations. By being present, making conscious choices, and finding satisfaction in the overall eating experience, individuals can navigate these occasions in a way that supports their well-being and enjoyment.

5. Health Benefits of the Mediterranean Diet

5.1 Weight Management

Weight management is the process of achieving and maintaining a healthy body weight through a combination of mindful eating, regular physical activity, and overall lifestyle choices. It involves finding a balance between energy intake (through food and beverages) and energy expenditure (through physical activity and bodily functions).

Maintaining a healthy weight is important for overall well-being and can have a positive impact on various aspects of health, including cardiovascular health, blood sugar regulation, and psychological well-being.

Weight management involves adopting a holistic approach that goes beyond solely focusing on the number on the scale. It includes developing sustainable habits and attitudes towards food, physical activity, and self-care.

Mindful eating plays a significant role in weight management. It involves paying attention to hunger and satiety cues, eating with awareness, and cultivating a positive relationship with food. Mindful eating emphasizes the enjoyment and satisfaction of meals, recognizing the body's signals of hunger and fullness, and making conscious choices that nourish the body.

Regular physical activity is essential for weight management. Engaging in activities that promote cardiovascular fitness, strength, and flexibility can help burn calories, build lean muscle mass, and support overall health. Finding enjoyable forms of exercise and incorporating them into daily routines is key to establishing a sustainable and balanced approach to physical activity.

Weight management also involves adopting lifestyle habits that support a healthy weight. This includes getting adequate sleep, managing stress levels, and practicing self-care. Sleep deprivation and chronic stress can affect hormonal balance and increase the risk of weight gain. Prioritizing self-care activities, such as relaxation techniques, hobbies, and social connections, contributes to overall well-being and helps manage emotional eating triggers.

It is important to note that weight management is highly individual and can vary based on factors such as age, genetics, and underlying health conditions. Consulting with healthcare professionals, registered dietitians, or qualified professionals can provide personalized guidance and support.

Sustainable weight management is not about quick fixes or drastic measures. It is a long-term commitment to adopting healthy habits and making gradual, lasting changes. It involves finding a balance that works for each individual's unique needs and preferences, focusing on overall health and well-being rather than solely on achieving a specific weight goal.

In summary, weight management is a holistic approach that involves mindful eating, regular physical activity, and overall lifestyle choices. It goes beyond solely focusing on weight and emphasizes overall well-being. Developing sustainable habits and attitudes towards food, physical activity, and self-care contribute to a balanced approach to weight management. Consulting with healthcare professionals and adopting an individualized approach is key to success in achieving and maintaining a healthy weight.

5.2 Heart Health

Heart health refers to the overall well-being and optimal functioning of the heart and circulatory system. It encompasses a range of factors that contribute to maintaining a healthy cardiovascular system and reducing the risk of heart disease.

A healthy heart is vital for overall health, as it is responsible for pumping oxygen-rich blood throughout the body. Promoting heart health involves adopting a lifestyle that supports the heart's functioning and reduces the risk of cardiovascular conditions such as heart attacks, strokes, and high blood pressure.

One key aspect of heart health is maintaining a balanced and nutritious diet. A heart-healthy diet typically includes an abundance of fruits, vegetables, whole grains, lean proteins, and healthy fats. This dietary pattern, such as the Mediterranean Diet, emphasizes the consumption of nutrient-rich foods that support cardiovascular health.

Regular physical activity is crucial for heart health. Engaging in aerobic exercises such as brisk walking, jogging, cycling, or swimming helps strengthen the heart muscle, improve circulation, and lower the risk of heart disease. Strength training exercises can also contribute to heart health by improving overall fitness and maintaining healthy body weight.

Managing and reducing stress levels is another important component of heart health. Chronic stress can contribute to the development of heart disease by raising blood pressure and increasing inflammation in the body. Engaging in stress-reducing activities, such as meditation, yoga, deep breathing exercises, or engaging in hobbies, can help promote relaxation and overall well-being.

Quitting smoking and avoiding exposure to secondhand smoke are vital for heart health. Smoking damages the blood vessels, raises blood pressure, and increases the risk of heart disease.

Quitting smoking significantly reduces the risk of heart-related problems and improves overall cardiovascular health.

Maintaining a healthy weight and managing chronic conditions, such as high blood pressure, diabetes, and high cholesterol, are essential for heart health. Excess weight, particularly around the waist, increases the risk of heart disease. Regular check-ups with healthcare professionals can help monitor and manage these conditions, reducing the risk of complications.

In summary, heart health encompasses a range of lifestyle factors that support the optimal functioning of the heart and reduce the risk of heart disease. A balanced and nutritious diet, regular physical activity, stress management, avoiding smoking, maintaining a healthy weight, and managing chronic conditions are all important elements of promoting heart health. By adopting these lifestyle practices, individuals can work towards maintaining a healthy cardiovascular system and reducing the risk of heart-related problems.

5.3 Diabetes Prevention and Management

Diabetes prevention and management involve strategies aimed at reducing the risk of developing diabetes or effectively managing the condition for those already diagnosed. Diabetes is a chronic metabolic disorder characterized by high blood sugar levels due to impaired insulin production or insulin resistance.

Prevention of diabetes is focused on adopting a healthy lifestyle that includes regular physical activity, maintaining a balanced diet, achieving and maintaining a healthy weight, and managing stress levels. Engaging in regular physical activity, such as brisk walking, jogging, or cycling, can improve insulin sensitivity and help prevent the onset of type 2 diabetes. A balanced diet that includes whole grains, lean proteins, fruits, vegetables, and healthy fats can support weight management, blood sugar control, and overall health.

For individuals already diagnosed with diabetes, effective management involves self-care practices and medical interventions. Self-care practices include monitoring blood sugar levels, adhering to a prescribed meal plan, managing carbohydrate intake, incorporating regular physical activity, and taking prescribed medications as directed. Regular monitoring of blood sugar levels helps individuals make informed decisions about food choices, physical activity, and medication management.

Proper nutrition plays a crucial role in diabetes management. Consistently following a balanced meal plan that includes carbohydrates, proteins, fats, and fiber helps maintain stable blood sugar levels. It is important to consume carbohydrates in moderation, focusing on complex carbohydrates with a lower glycemic index. Portion control and mindful eating are also key in managing diabetes, as they help maintain appropriate blood sugar levels and support weight management.

Diabetes management also involves regular medical check-ups and consultations with healthcare professionals. These professionals provide guidance, monitor blood sugar levels, adjust medication regimens if necessary, and offer support in managing the condition. Diabetes education programs and support groups can also be valuable resources for individuals to learn about self-management techniques, coping strategies, and lifestyle modifications.

Diabetes prevention and management require an individualized approach, considering factors such as age, overall health, and individual goals. Working closely with healthcare professionals, including physicians, registered dietitians, and diabetes educators, can provide personalized support and guidance.

In summary, diabetes prevention and management involve adopting a healthy lifestyle that includes regular physical activity, a balanced diet, weight management, stress reduction, and regular medical care. Prevention strategies focus on reducing the risk of developing diabetes, while management techniques aim to effectively control blood sugar levels and minimize complications for those already diagnosed. By embracing these strategies and working closely with healthcare professionals, individuals can take proactive steps towards preventing diabetes or managing the condition effectively.

5.4 Brain Health and Cognitive Function

Brain health and cognitive function are interconnected aspects of overall well-being that relate to the optimal functioning of the brain and its ability to perform cognitive tasks. The brain is a complex organ responsible for processing information, controlling bodily functions, and regulating emotions.

Maintaining brain health is important for supporting cognitive abilities such as memory, attention, problem-solving, and decision-making. It involves adopting a holistic approach that encompasses various lifestyle factors.

Physical activity plays a crucial role in brain health. Regular exercise promotes healthy blood flow and oxygenation to the brain, supports the growth and connectivity of neurons, and stimulates the release of beneficial chemicals in the brain. Engaging in aerobic exercises, strength training, and activities that challenge the brain, such as puzzles or learning new skills, can help enhance cognitive function and preserve brain health.

A balanced and nutritious diet is essential for brain health. Consuming a variety of nutrient-rich foods, including fruits, vegetables, whole grains, lean proteins, and healthy fats, provides the necessary vitamins, minerals, and antioxidants that support brain function. Specific nutrients, such as omega-3 fatty acids found in fatty fish, have been associated with improved cognitive performance.

Maintaining a healthy weight and managing chronic conditions, such as diabetes or high blood pressure, are important for brain health. These conditions can negatively impact brain function and increase the risk of cognitive decline. It is crucial to work with healthcare professionals to manage these conditions effectively and minimize their impact on brain health.

Mental and social stimulation also contribute to brain health. Engaging in intellectually stimulating activities, such as reading, learning new skills, or engaging in hobbies, helps keep the brain active and can support cognitive function. Social interactions and maintaining a strong social network are associated with better cognitive health and reduced risk of cognitive decline.

Quality sleep is essential for brain health and cognitive function. During sleep, the brain undergoes important processes that contribute to memory consolidation, neural repair, and overall brain health. Prioritizing sufficient sleep and practicing good sleep hygiene habits can support optimal brain function.

Stress management is crucial for brain health, as chronic stress can negatively impact cognitive function. Engaging in stress-reducing activities, such as relaxation techniques, mindfulness practices, or engaging in hobbies, helps promote overall well-being and supports brain health.

In summary, brain health and cognitive function are essential aspects of overall well-being. Adopting a holistic approach that includes regular physical activity, a balanced and nutritious diet, weight management, mental and social stimulation, quality sleep, and stress management can support optimal brain health. Nurturing brain health throughout life helps preserve cognitive function and promotes overall quality of life.

5.5 Cancer Prevention

Cancer prevention involves strategies and lifestyle choices aimed at reducing the risk of developing cancer. It focuses on adopting a proactive approach to minimize exposure to known risk factors and promoting overall health and well-being.

One key aspect of cancer prevention is maintaining a healthy lifestyle. This includes adopting a balanced and nutritious diet that is rich in fruits, vegetables, whole grains, lean proteins, and healthy fats. Such a diet provides essential nutrients, antioxidants, and phytochemicals that help support the body's natural defense mechanisms and reduce the risk of certain cancers.

Regular physical activity is also important for cancer prevention. Engaging in moderate to vigorous physical activity, such as brisk walking, jogging, cycling, or swimming, can help maintain a healthy weight, reduce inflammation, improve hormonal balance, and support overall well-being. Physical activity is known to be associated with a lower risk of certain cancers, including breast, colon, and lung cancer.

Avoiding tobacco in all forms is one of the most crucial steps in cancer prevention. Tobacco use is a major risk factor for several types of cancer, including lung, mouth, throat, and bladder cancer. Quitting smoking and avoiding exposure to secondhand smoke can significantly reduce the risk of developing these cancers.

Limiting alcohol consumption is another important aspect of cancer prevention. Excessive alcohol intake is associated with an increased risk of various cancers, including those of the breast, liver, mouth, throat, and esophagus. For those who choose to drink alcohol, moderate consumption is recommended, which means up to one drink per day for women and up to two drinks per day for men.

Protection from the harmful effects of ultraviolet (UV) radiation is crucial in preventing skin cancer. This involves avoiding excessive sun exposure, seeking shade, wearing protective clothing, and using sunscreen with a high sun protection factor (SPF). Regular skin self-examinations and routine skin screenings by healthcare professionals are also recommended for early detection of skin cancer.

Regular check-ups and screenings are essential for cancer prevention. These may include screenings for breast, cervical, colorectal, and prostate cancers, depending on age, gender, and individual risk factors. Routine examinations and early detection can significantly improve treatment outcomes and reduce mortality rates.

It is important to note that individual genetic predispositions and family history can influence cancer risk. For individuals with known genetic mutations or strong family histories of certain cancers, genetic counseling and personalized screening recommendations may be warranted.

In summary, cancer prevention involves adopting a proactive approach through lifestyle choices and strategies aimed at reducing the risk of developing cancer. This includes maintaining a healthy lifestyle, engaging in regular physical activity, avoiding tobacco and excessive alcohol consumption, protecting against UV radiation, and undergoing routine screenings. By embracing these strategies, individuals can take steps towards minimizing their cancer risk and promoting overall health and well-being.

5.6 Longevity and Aging

Longevity and aging are interconnected concepts that revolve around the process of growing older and the pursuit of living a long and fulfilling life. Longevity refers to the length of an individual's lifespan, while aging encompasses the physical, cognitive, and social changes that occur as we grow older.

Advances in healthcare and improvements in living conditions have contributed to increased life expectancy in many parts of the world. Longevity is influenced by various factors, including genetics, lifestyle choices, socioeconomic factors, access to healthcare, and environmental factors.

Aging is a natural and complex process that affects every individual differently. It involves physical changes, such as wrinkles, gray hair, and changes in bodily functions. Cognitive abilities may also change over time, with some individuals experiencing mild cognitive decline while others maintain their cognitive abilities well into old age. Socially, aging can bring new opportunities, such as retirement and spending time with family, as well as challenges related to social connections and support systems.

Promoting healthy aging involves adopting a holistic approach that encompasses various aspects of life. This includes maintaining a healthy lifestyle, engaging in regular physical activity, eating a balanced diet, getting sufficient sleep, managing stress levels, and avoiding harmful behaviors such as smoking or excessive alcohol consumption.

Staying mentally and socially active is also important for healthy aging. Engaging in cognitive activities, such as puzzles, reading, or learning new skills, helps keep the mind sharp. Social interactions, participation in community activities, and maintaining strong social connections contribute to overall well-being and a sense of purpose.

Access to quality healthcare is crucial for supporting healthy aging. Regular check-ups, preventive screenings, and appropriate medical interventions can help detect and manage age-related conditions and promote overall health. Healthcare professionals can provide guidance and personalized recommendations to address specific health concerns and optimize well-being.

Attitudes and perspectives towards aging also play a significant role. Embracing a positive mindset, cultivating resilience, and adapting to changes that come with aging contribute to overall well-being and satisfaction in later life. Emphasizing the value and wisdom that come with age can promote a healthy and positive perspective on the aging process.

It is important to note that aging is a highly individualized experience. Each person's journey is unique, influenced by a combination of genetic, environmental, and lifestyle factors. There is no one-size-fits-all approach to aging, and it is essential to respect and honor the diversity of experiences and challenges faced by individuals as they grow older.

In summary, longevity and aging encompass the length of life and the changes experienced as individuals grow older. Promoting healthy aging involves adopting a holistic approach that includes maintaining a healthy lifestyle, staying mentally and socially active, accessing quality healthcare, and cultivating positive attitudes towards aging. Embracing the journey of aging with grace and resilience contributes to overall well-being and the pursuit of a long and fulfilling life.

6. Modifying the Mediterranean Diet for Special Considerations
6.1 Vegetarian and Vegan Adaptations

Vegetarian and vegan adaptations involve dietary choices that exclude or minimize the consumption of animal products. These dietary approaches have gained popularity for various reasons, including ethical, environmental, and health considerations.

A vegetarian diet eliminates meat, poultry, and seafood from the diet, but may include other animal-derived products such as dairy, eggs, and honey. This dietary choice allows individuals to obtain essential nutrients from plant-based sources while still incorporating some animal products.

On the other hand, a vegan diet takes vegetarianism a step further by excluding all animal products, including dairy, eggs, honey, and even ingredients derived from animals, such as gelatin or certain food additives. Vegans rely solely on plant-based sources for their nutritional needs.

Both vegetarian and vegan diets can be nutritionally balanced when properly planned. It is essential to ensure an adequate intake of protein, iron, calcium, vitamin B12, omega-3 fatty acids, and other essential nutrients that may be obtained from animal sources. Plant-based protein sources include legumes, tofu, tempeh, seitan, nuts, and seeds, while iron-rich foods include dark leafy greens, legumes, and fortified cereals. Calcium can be sourced from plant-based foods like leafy greens, tofu, fortified plant-based milk, and certain nuts and seeds. Vitamin B12, primarily found in animal products, is important for vegans and can be obtained through fortified foods or supplements. Omega-3 fatty acids can be found in flaxseeds, chia seeds, walnuts, and algae-based supplements.

Vegetarian and vegan adaptations can offer several potential benefits. They promote the consumption of nutrient-dense plant foods such as fruits, vegetables, whole grains, legumes, and nuts, which are rich in fiber, vitamins, minerals, and beneficial plant compounds. These diets may contribute to a reduced risk of chronic diseases such as heart disease, high blood pressure, type 2 diabetes, and certain cancers.

Moreover, vegetarian and vegan choices can have positive environmental impacts. The production of animal products is often associated with higher greenhouse gas emissions, land and water use, and deforestation. By reducing or eliminating the consumption of animal products, individuals can contribute to sustainable food systems and the preservation of natural resources.

It is important to note that vegetarian and vegan adaptations are not suitable for everyone. Individual nutritional needs, health conditions, and personal preferences should be considered. Some individuals may find it necessary to consult with healthcare professionals or registered dietitians to ensure they are meeting their nutritional requirements and maintaining overall health.

In summary, vegetarian and vegan adaptations involve dietary choices that limit or eliminate the consumption of animal products. When properly planned, these dietary approaches can provide balanced nutrition and offer potential health benefits.

They also align with sustainability goals by reducing the environmental impact of food choices. However, individual considerations and nutritional needs should be taken into account to ensure a healthy and well-rounded plant-based diet.

6.2 Gluten-Free Options

Gluten-free options refer to food choices that do not contain gluten, a protein found in wheat, barley, rye, and their derivatives. For individuals with gluten-related disorders, such as celiac disease or gluten sensitivity, following a gluten-free diet is essential to avoid adverse health effects.

Celiac disease is an autoimmune condition in which the immune system reacts to gluten, damaging the lining of the small intestine. This can lead to various symptoms, including gastrointestinal issues, nutrient deficiencies, fatigue, and other systemic effects. Gluten sensitivity, also known as non-celiac gluten sensitivity, is a less severe condition in which individuals experience symptoms similar to celiac disease without the same immune response.

A gluten-free diet requires eliminating all sources of gluten from the diet. This means avoiding obvious sources like bread, pasta, cereals, and baked goods made with wheat, barley, or rye flour. Additionally, individuals following a gluten-free diet need to be vigilant about hidden sources of gluten in processed foods, condiments, sauces, and even certain medications and supplements.

To replace gluten-containing grains, gluten-free options often rely on alternative grains, starches, and flours. Common gluten-free grains include rice, corn, quinoa, millet, and sorghum. These grains can be used as substitutes in various dishes, such as gluten-free pasta, bread, and baked goods.

Other gluten-free starches and flours, such as potato starch, tapioca starch, and almond flour, are commonly used in gluten-free cooking and baking. These ingredients help provide structure, texture, and flavor to gluten-free recipes.

It is important to note that naturally gluten-free foods, such as fruits, vegetables, legumes, dairy products, and most meats, are suitable for individuals following a gluten-free diet. However, cross-contamination should be considered, especially in food preparation and cooking surfaces, to avoid unintentional exposure to gluten.

Gluten-free options have become more widely available in recent years, with an increasing number of gluten-free products and dedicated gluten-free food brands. However, it is essential to read labels carefully and look for certifications to ensure that products are truly gluten-free and have not been contaminated during processing.

While a gluten-free diet is necessary for individuals with gluten-related disorders, it is not recommended for those without a medical need. Gluten-containing grains are generally nutritious and provide important nutrients, including fiber, vitamins, and minerals. Removing gluten from the diet without medical necessity may result in nutrient deficiencies if not adequately balanced and monitored.

In summary, gluten-free options are food choices that do not contain gluten and are necessary for individuals with gluten-related disorders. A gluten-free diet involves eliminating gluten-containing grains and substituting them with alternative grains, starches, and flours. It is important to read labels carefully and ensure that products are certified gluten-free. For individuals without a medical need, a gluten-free diet is not necessary and may lead to nutrient deficiencies if not properly balanced.

6.3 Mediterranean Diet for Pregnancy and Childhood

The Mediterranean diet is a dietary pattern traditionally followed in the countries bordering the Mediterranean Sea. It is characterized by an abundance of fruits, vegetables, whole grains, legumes, nuts, and seeds, along with moderate consumption of fish, poultry, dairy products, and eggs. It is also known for its emphasis on healthy fats, such as olive oil, and moderate consumption of red wine.

The Mediterranean diet is considered a healthy eating pattern for individuals of all ages, including pregnant women and children.

During pregnancy, following a balanced and nutritious diet is crucial for the health and development of both the mother and the baby. The Mediterranean diet provides a wide range of essential nutrients, including vitamins, minerals, healthy fats, and antioxidants, which are important for fetal growth and development.

The abundance of fruits and vegetables in the Mediterranean diet provides important vitamins, minerals, and fiber, promoting overall health and supporting healthy digestion. These foods are also rich in antioxidants, which help protect against oxidative stress and inflammation.

Whole grains, such as whole wheat, brown rice, and oats, provide complex carbohydrates, fiber, and essential nutrients. They provide sustained energy and can help regulate blood sugar levels.

Legumes, including beans, lentils, and chickpeas, are excellent sources of plant-based protein, fiber, and various micronutrients. They contribute to satiety, help maintain stable blood sugar levels, and support overall health.

The Mediterranean diet also includes moderate amounts of fish, which is a rich source of omega-3 fatty acids, essential for fetal brain and eye development. However, pregnant women should be cautious about consuming fish with high levels of mercury and should follow local guidelines regarding safe seafood consumption.

Poultry, dairy products, and eggs are included in moderation, providing additional sources of protein, calcium, and other essential nutrients. Choosing lean poultry cuts, low-fat dairy options, and eggs from a reliable source can help meet nutrient needs while minimizing saturated fat intake.

While red wine is a component of the Mediterranean diet, it is important to note that alcohol consumption during pregnancy is not recommended due to potential risks to the developing baby. Pregnant women should avoid alcohol completely.

In childhood, following a Mediterranean-style diet can support healthy growth and development. It encourages the consumption of nutrient-dense foods, limits highly processed and sugary foods, and promotes a balanced approach to eating.

The Mediterranean diet for children emphasizes whole foods, such as fruits, vegetables, whole grains, and legumes, which provide essential nutrients for growth, development, and optimal immune function. Encouraging a variety of flavors and textures from different food groups can help children develop a diverse and nutritious diet.

The inclusion of healthy fats, such as olive oil, nuts, and seeds, supports brain development and cognitive function in children. These fats also provide satiety and contribute to the absorption of fat-soluble vitamins.

Promoting regular physical activity and a positive mealtime environment are also important aspects of fostering healthy eating habits in childhood. It is beneficial to involve children in meal preparation and educate them about the importance of a balanced diet, while also respecting their individual preferences and appetites.

In summary, the Mediterranean diet is a healthy eating pattern that can be adapted for pregnancy and childhood. It provides a variety of nutrient-dense foods, promotes a balanced approach to eating, and emphasizes the importance of healthy fats and whole foods. However, it is important to consult with healthcare professionals, registered dietitians, or pediatricians for personalized guidance and recommendations specific to individual needs and circumstances.

6.4 Mediterranean Diet for Athletes

The Mediterranean diet is a dietary pattern that can be beneficial for athletes due to its emphasis on whole, minimally processed foods and its inclusion of nutrient-dense ingredients. This eating pattern, traditionally followed in Mediterranean countries, provides a balanced combination of carbohydrates, proteins, and healthy fats, along with a wide array of vitamins, minerals, and antioxidants.

Carbohydrates are a key component of the Mediterranean diet and serve as the primary source of energy for athletes. Whole grains, fruits, and vegetables are rich in complex carbohydrates, providing sustained energy for training and exercise. These foods also contain fiber, which aids in digestion and helps regulate blood sugar levels.

Proteins play a vital role in muscle repair and recovery. The Mediterranean diet includes moderate amounts of lean proteins, such as fish, poultry, legumes, and dairy products, which can support muscle growth and repair. Athletes may consider incorporating a variety of protein sources to ensure they meet their individual needs.

Healthy fats, such as those found in olive oil, nuts, seeds, and fatty fish, are important for athletes' overall health and performance. These fats provide essential fatty acids and fat-soluble vitamins, help reduce inflammation, and support cardiovascular health. Including moderate amounts of these healthy fats can contribute to optimal athletic performance.

Fruits and vegetables are abundant in the Mediterranean diet, providing athletes with important vitamins, minerals, and antioxidants. These nutrients are essential for immune function, recovery, and overall health. Additionally, the antioxidants found in fruits and vegetables help combat oxidative stress, which can be increased during intense physical activity.

Hydration is crucial for athletes, and the Mediterranean diet promotes the consumption of water as the primary beverage. Staying adequately hydrated is essential for maintaining performance, regulating body temperature, and supporting overall bodily functions.

The Mediterranean diet also allows for occasional consumption of red wine in moderation. However, it is important for athletes to understand that alcohol can have negative effects on hydration, recovery, and performance, and it should be consumed sparingly or avoided altogether, especially around training or competition.

Each athlete has unique nutritional needs based on factors such as training intensity, duration, and individual goals. It is important for athletes to work with registered dietitians or sports nutrition professionals who can provide personalized guidance and recommendations tailored to their specific needs and sport.

In summary, the Mediterranean diet can provide a solid foundation for athletes by emphasizing whole, nutrient-dense foods. It offers a balanced combination of carbohydrates, proteins, and healthy fats, along with a wide range of vitamins, minerals, and antioxidants. However, individual needs and goals should be considered, and athletes should seek professional guidance to optimize their nutrition and fuel their performance effectively.

BREAKFAST RECIPES

Chickpea egg bowl
Serves: 3 **Time:** 35 Minutes

Ingredients:

2 Boiled Eggs, Large and Chopped

2 Tablespoons Parsley, Fresh and Chopped Fine

1 green onion, Chopped Fine

1 Tablespoon juice, Fresh

1 Cup Chickpeas, Rinsed and Drained

Preparation:

1. Add your chickpeas and 1 ½ cups of water into your moment pot and mix in your Ingredients. Ensure its blended well, and afterwards cook on high pressing factor for 12 minutes.

2. Allow the Ingredients to cook and snappy delivery, and afterwards blend in your excess Ingredients. Serve warm.

Wholesome Info per Servings:

Calories: 267, Protein: 14 g, Fat: 6 g, Carbs: 34 g, Sodium: 53 mg

New Cheese with Tomato

Serves: 2 **Time:** quarter-hour

Ingredients:

1/4 Teaspoon wine Vinegar

2 Tomatoes, Chopped

1 Tablespoon vegetable oil

¼ Cup pot cheese

Ocean Salt and Black Pepper to taste

Preparation:

1. Add your tomatoes during a blender and puree until smooth.

2. Add in your excess Ingredients apart from the oil, and blend to form it smooth.

3. Take your moment pot and press sauté. When it's hot, include your oil.

4. Add your tomato blend in, and cook for 3 to four minutes.

5. Add them to the Cooking pot, and join well. Serve warm.

Wholesome Info per Servings: Calories: 84, Protein: 4 Grams, Fat: 7 Grams, Carbs: 2 Grams, Sodium: 121 mg

Broccoli and Eggs

Serves: 4 **Time:** 40 Minutes

Ingredients:

1 Onion, Chopped

6 Eggs, Beaten

1 Tablespoon All-Purpose Flour

1 lb. Broccoli, Chopped into Florets

Preparation:

1. Mix your eggs, flavours and flour during a blending bowl and afterwards include your broccoli. Throw to hide, and afterwards set it aside.

2. Line a preparing dish with material paper and oil it with a Cooking splash.

Include your broccoli.

3. Pour some water into the instant pot, and afterwards, include your liner crate.

4. Arrange your container within the crate, and afterwards, close the duvet.

5. Cook on high pressing factor for thirty minutes, and afterwards, fast delivery.

6. Serve warm.

Healthful Info per Servings:

Calories: 160, Protein: 13 Grams, Fat: 8 Grams, Carbs: 10 Grams, Sodium: 147 mg

Garlic eggs
Serves: 4 **Time:** 25 Minute

Ingredients:

1 Tablespoon vegetable oil

6 Tomatoes, Small

4 Eggs

1 Teaspoon Garlic, Minced

1 Teaspoon Turmeric Powder

1 scallion, Chopped

Ocean Salt and Black Pepper to taste

Preparation:

1. Halve your tomatoes, and afterwards, set them aside.

2. Place a tablespoon of vegetable oil into your moment pot and press sauté before adding your tomatoes. Put the cut side down, and afterwards, add in your garlic and turmeric.

3. Add in your eggs, and blend them with a spatula to scramble. Season with salt and pepper.

4. Cook for around a quarter-hour, and sprinkle with slashed scallion to serve.

Wholesome Info per Servings: Calories: 118, Protein: 6.7 Grams, Fat: 8.2 Grams, Carbs: 5.7 Grams, Sodium: 68 mg

Banana quinoa
Serves: 3 **Time:** 20 Minutes

Ingredients:

¾ Cup Quinoa, Soaked in Water for 1 Hour

8 Ounces Almond Milk, Canned

¾ Cup Water

1 Teaspoon vanilla, unadulterated

½ Cup Banana, Peeled and Sliced

1 Pinch Sea Salt Topping:

6 Banana Slices

Chocolate, Grated (Optional)

Preparation:

1. Add all of your quinoa Ingredients to the instant pot and secure the highest.

Press rice, and afterwards cook for twelve minutes on low pressing factor.

2. Release the pressing factor normally and afterwards mix. The spot in serving bowls and top with banana and chocolate.

Healthful Info per Servings: Calories: 371, Protein: 7.3 Grams, Fat: 20.4 Grams, Carbs: 41.4 Grams, Sodium: 17.4 mg

Almond risotto

Serves: 3 **Time:** quarter-hour

Ingredients:

2 Cups Almond Milk, Vanilla

2 Tablespoons Honey, Raw

1 Teaspoon vanilla, Pure

¼ Cup Almond Flakes, Toasted for Garnish

½ Cup Arborio Rice

Preparation:

1. Place everything of your Ingredients into the instant pot, and afterwards cook on high pressing factor for five minutes.

2. leave a characteristic pressing factor delivery and serve embellished with almond drops.

Nourishing Info per Servings:

Calories: 116, Protein: 2 Grams, Fat: 2.1 Grams, Carbs: 22.5 Grams, Sodium: 82 mg

Coconut risotto

Serves: 3 **Time:** quarter-hour

Ingredients:

2 Cups Coconut Milk

½ Cup Arborio Rice

2 Tablespoons Coconut Sugar

1 teaspoon vanilla

¼ Cup Coconut Flakes, Toasted for Garnish

Preparation:

1. Throw everything of your Ingredients into the instant pot and afterwards cook on high pressing factor for five minutes.

2. leave a characteristic pressing factor discharge for twenty minutes before presenting with coconut drops.

Dietary Info per Servings:

Calories: 532, Protein: 5.9 Grams, Fat: 40.4 Grams, Carbs: 42.1 Grams, Sodium: 25 mg

Breakfast quinoa

Serves: 4 **Time:** quarter-hour

Ingredients:

1 cup Quinoa, Rinsed and Drained

3 Cups Almond Milk, Vanilla ¼ Cup Almonds

1 Cup Blackberries, Chopped

¼ Teaspoon Cinnamon

Preparation:

1. tart by setting your quinoa in your moment pot, and afterwards, pour in your milk. Include your cinnamon. Seal your moment pot before setting it to manual settings.

2. Cook at high pressing factor for 2 minutes before considering a characteristic pressing factor discharge.

3. Top with almonds and berries before serving.

Wholesome Info per Servings: Calories: 267, Protein: 8.5 Grams, Fat: 7.6 Grams, Carbs: 35 Grams, Sodium: 140 Grams

Coconut yoghurt

Serves: 4

Time: 12 Hours half-hour

Ingredients:

1 Tablespoon Gelatine

3 cups of coconut milk

1 Package Yoghurt Starter

Preparation:

1. Start by including your coconut milk in your moment pot before squeezing the yoghurt setting.

2. Remove the pot and switch it off.

3. Allow it to chill within the cooler for ten minutes before moving onto the subsequent stage.

4. Afterwards, mix in your yoghurt starter until it's smooth, and set your pot back to your moment pot.

5. Press your yoghurt button another time, setting the prospect to eight hours. Mix in your gelatine bit by bit.

6. Refrigerate for in any event four hours before serving.

Healthful Info per Servings:

Calories: 421, Protein: 5.6 Grams, Fat: 42.9 Grams, Carbs: 10.2 Grams, Sodium: 32 mg

Squash and Apple Porridge

Serves: 4 **Time:** 20 Minutes

Ingredients:

1 Delicate Squash, Peeled

4 Apples, Cored and Sliced

1/8 Teaspoon Ground Ginger

½ Teaspoon Cinnamon

2 Tablespoons syrup

Preparation:

1. Start by putting your apples and squash in your moment pot before including some water.

2. Sprinkle with ginger, a scramble of salt and cinnamon before fixing your pot and setting it to manual. Cook on high pressing factor for eight minutes.

3. leave a characteristic pressing factor delivery and afterwards cut the squash.

4. Transfer your squash and every one the opposite things during a blender, beating until smooth.

5. Drizzle with syrup before serving.

Healthful Info per Servings: Calories: 151, Protein: 1.2 Grams, Fat: 0.5 Grams, Carbs: 39.4 Grams, Sodium: 48 mg

Strawberry-Thyme Millet Bowl

Preparation Time: 15 minutes

Cooking Time: 20 minutes

Servings: 1

Ingredients:

One lb. strawberries, hulled and halved

Four sprigs of fresh thyme

1 1/2 tsp. pure vanilla extract

2 tbsp. finely chopped pistachios

2 tbsp. hemp seeds

1 tbsp. olive oil

1 tbsp. honey

One c. 2% milk, plus more for serving

One c. millet

Directions:

Ø Preheat the oven to 450°F. Toss strawberries, thyme, oil, and honey on a rimmed baking sheet—roast for about 10 minutes or until the berries start to release juices. Remove the thyme from the oven and set it aside.

Ø Meanwhile, bring milk and 1 cup water to a boil in a saucepan. Stir in the millet and vanilla, then lower to low heat and cover for 25 to 30 minutes, or until the millet is soft and the liquid has been absorbed.

Millet should be served with berries and pan juices, a splash of milk, pistachios, and hemp seeds.

Blueberry Smoothie Bowl

Preparation Time: 15 minutes

Cooking Time: 20 minutes

Servings: 1

Ingredients:

One c. frozen blueberries

1/2 c. unsweetened almond milk

1/4 c. vanilla granola

2 tbsp. sliced almonds

2 tsp. hemp seeds

1 tsp. ground cinnamon

1 1/2 scoops protein powder

2 tbsp. unsweetened almond butter

1 tsp. pure vanilla extract

1/2 c. fresh blueberries

Directions:

Ø Puree frozen blueberries, almond milk, protein powder, almond butter, and vanilla in a blender until smooth. Divide the mixture into two bowls.

Ø Before serving, top each bowl with fresh blueberries, granola, almonds, hemp seeds, and cinnamon.

Cauliflower "Tabbouleh."
Preparation Time: 15 minutes

Cooking Time: 20 minutes

Servings: 1

Ingredients:

1/2 small red onion, finely chopped

1/2 tsp. ground cumin

1/2 tsp. kosher salt

1/2 tsp. pepper

12 oz. raw cauliflower florets

One packed c. curly parsley (including stems), chopped One c. mixed-color cherry tomatoes halved

2 Persian cucumbers, sliced

3 tbsp. fresh lemon juice

Directions:

Ø To make cauliflower rice, pulse cauliflower in a food processor until very finely diced (you should have around 2 1/2 cups). Transfer to a large mixing bowl.

Ø In the same food processor dish, Parsley pulse until very finely chopped. Combine cauliflower, cherry tomatoes, cucumbers, lemon juice, red onion, ground cumin, kosher salt, and pepper in a mixing bowl. Toss to blend and taste for spices.

Scrambled Egg Tacos

Preparation Time: 15 minutes

Cooking Time: 20 minutes

Servings: 1

Ingredients:

2 tbsp. olive oil, divided

One 15-oz. can of black beans, rinsed

1/2 tsp. cumin seeds

1 tbsp. fresh lemon juice

Eight large eggs

Eight yellow corn tortillas

sour cream, for serving

crumbled queso fresco for serving

cilantro, for serving

One clove garlic, finely chopped

kosher salt

pepper

Four c. baby spinach

Directions:

Ø In a large skillet, heat one tablespoon of oil over medium heat.

Combine the beans, cumin, and garlic in a mixing bowl. Season with 1/8 teaspoon salt and pepper and sauté for 2 minutes, or until the garlic begins to turn golden brown. Remove from the fire and toss in the spinach until the leaves are wilted. Mix in the lemon juice.

Ø Whisk together eggs, 1 tbsp water, and 1/2 tsp salt and pepper in a mixing dish.

Ø Heat the remaining tbsp—oil in a medium nonstick skillet over medium heat. Cook, stirring with a rubber spatula every few seconds until the eggs are done to your liking, about 2 to 3 minutes for medium-soft eggs.

Ø Toasted tortillas should be lightly charred under the broiler or a gas flame. Fill tortillas with beans, eggs, sour cream, queso fresco, and, if preferred, cilantro.

Whipped Feta and Watermelon Radishes Toast
Preparation Time: 15 minutes

Cooking Time: 20 minutes

Servings: 1

Ingredients:

3 oz. feta cheese, broken into pieces

2 tbsp. milk

Four thick slices of sourdough toast

One medium watermelon radish, very thinly sliced kosher salt, for serving

pepper, for serving

Two red radishes, very thinly sliced

1/2 c. radish or broccoli sprouts

olive oil, for serving

Directions:

Ø Puree feta cheese and milk in a tiny food processor until smooth, adding extra milk if needed. Spread on pieces of bread: watermelon radish, red radishes, and radish or broccoli sprouts on top. Drizzle with olive oil and season with salt and pepper to taste.

Tomato Toasts with Mint Yogurt and Sumac Vinaigrette

Preparation Time: 15 minutes

Cooking Time: 20 minutes

Servings: 1

Ingredients:

1 tsp. lemon juice

1/4 tsp. cumin seed

1/4 tsp. ground sumac

1/4 tsp. coarsely cracked pepper

1/4 tsp. kosher salt

Four pieces toasted bread1/2 c. plain Greek yogurt One scallion, finely chopped, plus more for serving 1/4 c. mint, chopped

2 tsp. grated lemon zest

2 tbsp. olive oil

Three medium heirloom tomatoes, sliced

Directions:

Ø Combine Greek yogurt, scallions, mint, and lemon zest in a mixing dish.

Ø Whisk together the olive oil, lemon juice, cumin seed, crushed sumac, cracked pepper, and kosher salt in a separate bowl.

Ø Spread yogurt over toast, top with heirloom tomatoes, then drizzles with vinaigrette. If desired, top with extra chopped scallions.

Spinach and Goat Cheese Egg Muffins

Preparation Time: 15 minutes

Cooking Time: 20 minutes

Servings: 1

Ingredients:

1 tbsp. olive oil

One large red pepper, cut into 1/4-in. pieces

Kosher salt and pepper

1 5-oz. pkg. baby spinach, chopped

1/4 c. fresh goat cheese, crumbled

Two scallions, chopped

Six large eggs

1/2 c. milk

Directions:

Ø Preheat the oven to 350°F. Nonstick cooking spray should be sprayed onto a 12-cup muffin tray.

Ø In a large skillet over medium heat, heat the oil. Cook, covered, for 6 to 8 minutes, until soft, with red pepper and 18 tsp each salt and pepper. Remove from the heat and add the scallions.

Ø In a large mixing dish, combine eggs, milk, 14 teaspoon salt, and 18 teaspoon pepper. Stir in the spinach-red pepper combination.

Ø Divide mixture evenly among muffin cups (approximately 14 cups each), sprinkle with goat cheese, and bake for 20 to 25 minutes, or until just set in the middle. (The tops of the frittatas may appear moist from the spinach even after they have set.)

Ø Allow cooling for 5 minutes on a wire rack before removing from pan. Serve hot. Refrigerate for up to 4 days; reheat in a microwave for 30 seconds on high.

Best Ever Shakshuka

Preparation Time: 15 minutes

Cooking Time: 20 minutes

Servings: 1

Ingredients:

2 tbsp. olive oil

One onion, finely chopped

pepper

One lb. cherry and Campari tomatoes, halved if large Eight large eggs

1/4 c. fresh basil, finely chopped

toasted baguette, for serving

One clove garlic, finely chopped

1 tsp. ground cumin

kosher salt

Directions:

Ø Preheat the oven to 400°F. Heat the oil in a large oven-safe skillet over medium heat. Eight minutes later, the onion should be golden brown and soft—Cook for 1 minute after adding garlic, cumin, and ½ teaspoon salt and pepper. Stir in the tomatoes, then place in the oven for 10 minutes. Stir the veggies, form 8 tiny wells in the vegetable mixture and delicately crack one egg into each one. Return to oven and bake eggs until done to preference, 7 to 8 minutes for slightly runny yolks. Serve with bread and a sprinkle of basil.

Spinach-Curry Crepes with Apple, Raisins, and Chickpeas

Preparation Time: 15 minutes

Cooking Time: 20 minutes

Servings: 1

Ingredients:

One sum yellow onion, chopped

One can (15.5 oz) chickpeas, rinsed and drained

One granny smith apple, diced

1/4 C golden raisins

2 tbsp. madras curry powder

10 oz. fresh spinach

lemon wedges, for serving

Two LG eggs

1/3 C finely chopped fresh cilantro

1/4 tsp. black pepper

2 1/2 C 1% milk

1 C plus 2 tbsp all-purpose flour

3 tbsp. safflower oil

3/4 tsp. kosher salt

Directions:

Ø In a blender, combine the eggs, cilantro, pepper, 1 cup each of milk and flour, two tablespoons of oil, and 1/4 teaspoon salt. Coat a 10" nonstick skillet with cooking spray and heat over medium heat. Pour 1/3 cup batter equally into the pan and cook until sides are firm, about 1 minute—Cook for 30 seconds on the other side. Repeat with the remaining crepes. Keep warm by covering.

Ø Heat the remaining one tablespoon of oil in a pan over medium heat. Cook until the onion is tender, about 5 minutes. Combine the chickpeas, apple, raisins, and curry powder in a mixing bowl. Cook for 3 minutes. Cook for 30 seconds after adding the remaining 2 tbsp flour. Add the remaining 1 1/2 cups milk and mix well—Cook for 2 minutes, or until the sauce is thick. Stir in the spinach and the remaining ½ teaspoon salt—Cook for 2 minutes, or until the spinach has wilted. Divide the filling among the crepes, fold in half, and serve with lemon wedges.

Healthy Herb Frittata

Preparation Time: 15 minutes

Cooking Time: 20 minutes

Servings: 1

Ingredients:

1/4 c. crème fraî che, at room temp

2 tbsp. chopped chives

Six large eggs

4 tbsp. olive oil, divided

kosher salt

pepper

Six scallions, cut into 1-in. pieces

Two c. flat-leaf parsley leaves, plus more for sprinkling Two c. cilantro leaves and tender stems, plus more for sprinkling 1/2 c. dill fronds, plus more for sprinkling

Directions:

Ø Preheat the oven to 350°F. Combine crème fraîche and chives in a mixing bowl; set aside until ready to use. f. Lightly beat the egg in a separate basin. s. In a food processor, combine scallions, parsley, cilantro, dill, and two tablespoons of oil until equally and finely chopped. d. Combine a mixing dish with the eggs and 1/2 teaspoon salt and pepper to taste. f. Heat the remaining two tablespoons oil in a medium pan over medium heat until shimmering, approximately 2 minutes. n Cook until the edges of the egg mixture begin to sizzle and solidify for about 2 minutes. Place skillet in oven and bake for 18 to 20 minutes, or until center is just set. n. Rest for at least 5 mi. n. Serve with chive crème fraîche. If desired, top with more herbs. Red.

Skillet Eggplant & Kale Frittata
Servings:1

Cooking Time:20 Minutes

Ingredients:

1 tbsp olive oil

3 large eggs

1 tsp milk

1 cup curly kale, torn

½ eggplant, peeled and diced

¼ red bell pepper, chopped

Salt and black pepper to taste

1 oz crumbled Goat cheese

Directions:

1. Preheat your broiler. Whisk the eggs with milk, salt, and pepper until just combined. Heat the olive oil in a small skillet over medium heat. Spread the eggs on the bottom and add the kale on top in an even layer; top with veggies.

2. Season with salt and pepper. Allow the eggs and vegetables to cook 3 to 5 minutes until the bottom half of the eggs are firm and vegetables are tender. Top with the crumbled Goat cheese and place under the broiler for 5 minutes until the eggs are firm in the middle and the cheese has melted. Slice into wedges and serve immediately.

Nutrition Info: Per Serving: Calories: 622;Fat: 39g;Protein: 41g;Carbs: 33g.

Basic Tortilla De Patatas

Servings:4

Cooking Time:35 Minutes

Ingredients:

1 ½ lb gold potatoes, peeled and sliced

½ cup olive oil

1 sweet onion, thinly sliced

8 eggs

½ dried oregano

Salt to taste

Directions:

1. Heat the olive oil in a skillet over medium heat. Fry the potatoes for 8-10 minutes, stirring often. Add in onion, oregano, and salt and cook for 5-6 minutes until the potatoes are tender and slightly golden; set aside.

2. In a bowl, beat the eggs with a pinch of salt. Add in the potato mixture and mix well. Pour into the skillet and cook for about 10-12 minutes. Flip the tortilla using a plate, and cook for 2 more minutes until nice and crispy. Slice and serve.

Nutrition Info:Per Serving: Calories: 440;Fat: 34g;Protein: 14g;Carbs: 22g.

MEAT RECIPES

Beef Stew with Eggplants

Preparation Time: 15 minutes

Cooking Time: 10 hours

Servings: 2

Ingredients:

10 oz. of the beef neck, or another tender cut, chopped into bite-sized pieces

1 large eggplant, sliced

2 cups of fire-roasted tomatoes

½ cup of fresh green peas

1 cup of beef broth

4 tbsp. of olive oil

2 tbsp. of tomato paste

1 tbsp. of Cayenne pepper, ground

½ tsp of chili pepper, ground (optional)

½ tsp of salt

Parmesan cheese

Directions:

1. Grease the bottom of a slow cooker with olive oil. Toss all ingredients and add about 1-1 ½ cups of water. Cook within 8-10 hours on low, or until the meat is fork-tender. Sprinkle with Parmesan cheese before serving, but this is optional.

Nutrition: Calories 195 Proteins 15.3g Carbohydrates 9.6g Fat 11.1g 149.

Chopped Veal Kebab

Preparation Time: 15 minutes

Cooking Time: 10 hours

Servings: 5

Ingredients:

2 lb. boneless veal shoulder, cut into bite-sized pieces 3 large tomatoes, roughly chopped

2 tbsp. of all-purpose flour

3 tbsp. of butter

1 tbsp. of cayenne pepper

1 tsp of salt

1 tbsp. of parsley, finely chopped

1 cup of Greek yogurt (can be replaced with sour cream) for serving 1 pide bread (can be replaced with any bread you have on hand)

Directions:

1. Oil the bottom of your slow cooker with one tablespoon of butter.

2. Make a layer with veal chops and pour enough water to cover.

3. Season with salt and close the lid. Set to low and simmer within 8-10 hours. Remove, then transfer to a plate.

2. Dissolve the rest of the butter in a small skillet. Add one tablespoon of cayenne pepper, two tablespoons of all-purpose flour, and briefly stir-fry - for about two minutes. Remove from the heat.

3. Chop pide bread and arrange it on a serving plate. Place the meat and tomato on top. Drizzle with browned cayenne pepper, top with Greek yogurt, and sprinkle with chopped parsley. Serve immediately.

Nutrition: Calories 437 Proteins 49.7g Carbohydrates 8.9g Fat 21.8g

Garlic Meatballs

Preparation Time: 15 minutes

Cooking Time: 8 hours

Servings: 5

Ingredients:

1 lb. lean ground beef

7 oz. rice

2 small onions, peeled and finely chopped 2 garlic cloves, crushed 1 egg, beaten

1 large potato, peeled and sliced

3 tbsp. of extra virgin olive oil

1 tsp of salt

Directions:

1. Mix the lean ground beef with rice, finely chopped onions, crushed garlic, one beaten egg, and salt in a large bowl. Shape the batter into 15-20 meatballs.

2. Oiled the bottom of your slow cooker with three tablespoons of olive oil. Make the first layer with sliced potatoes and top with meatballs. Cook low within 6-8 hours.

Nutrition: Calories 468 Proteins 33g Carbohydrates 47g Fat 15.3g

Meat Pie with Yogurt

Preparation Time: 15 minutes

Cooking Time: 6 hours

Servings: 6

Ingredients:

2 lb. lean ground beef

5-6 garlic cloves, crushed

1 tsp of salt

½ tsp freshly ground black pepper

1 (16 oz.) pack of yufka dough

½ cup of butter, melted

1 cup of sour cream

3 cups of liquid yogurt

Directions:

1. Mix the ground beef with garlic cloves, salt, and pepper in a large bowl.

Mix well until fully incorporated. Lay a sheet of yufka on a work surface and brush with melted butter. Line with the meat mixture and roll up. Repeat the process until all fixing is used.

2. Gently place in a lightly greased slow cooker and close the lid.

1. Cook for 4-6 hours on low, remove from the cooker and allow it to cool. Meanwhile, combine sour cream with yogurt. Spread the mixture over the pie and serve cold.

Nutrition: Calories 503 Proteins 47.4g Carbohydrates 2.6g Fat 32.8g

Moussaka

Preparation Time: 15 minutes

Cooking Time: 8 hours

Servings: 5

Ingredients:

2 lb. large potatoes, peeled and sliced

1 lb. lean ground beef

1 large onion, peeled and finely chopped

1 tsp of salt

½ tsp of black pepper, ground

½ cup of milk

2 large eggs, beaten

Vegetable oil

Sour cream or Greek yogurt for serving

Directions:

1. Grease the bottom of your cooker with some vegetable oil. Make one layer with sliced potatoes and brush with some milk. Spread the ground beef and make another layer with potatoes. Brush with the remaining milk, add ½ cup of water, and close the lid.

2. Cook within 8 hours on low or 4-6 hours on high. When done, make the final layer with a beaten egg. Cover the cooker and let it stand for about 10 minutes. Top with some sour cream or Greek yogurt, and serve!

Nutrition: Calories 458 Proteins 34.9g Carbohydrates 36g Fat 19.2g

Pepper Meat

Preparation Time: 15 minutes

Cooking Time: 10 hours

Servings: 6

Ingredients:

2 lbs. of beef fillet or another tender cut

5 medium-sized onions, peeled and finely chopped 3 tbsp. of tomato paste

2 tbsp. of oil

1 tbsp. of butter, melted

2 tbsp. of fresh parsley, finely chopped

½ tsp of freshly ground black pepper

1 tsp of salt

Directions:

1. Oiled the bottom of your slow cooker with some oil. About two tablespoons will be enough. Slice the meat into bite-sized and place them in the cooker.

2. Add finely chopped onions, tomato paste, fresh parsley, salt, and pepper. Mix and put about 2 cups of water. Cook on low for 8-10 hours. Stir in one tablespoon of melted butter and serve warm.

Nutrition: Calories 382 Proteins 47.3g Carbohydrates 10.3g Fat 16g 154.

Roast Lamb

Preparation Time: 15 minutes

Cooking Time: 8 hours

Servings: 5

Ingredients:

2 lb. lamb leg

3 tbsp. extra virgin olive oil

2 tsp salt

Directions:

1. Grease the bottom of a slow cooker with three tablespoons of olive oil.

Rinse and generously season the meat with salt and place it in the cooker. Cook on low within one hour on high and 6-7 hours on low, or until the meat is tender and separates from the bones.

Nutrition: Calories 473 Proteins 49.7g Carbohydrates 8.9g Fat 21.8g

Rosemary Meatballs

Preparation Time: 15 minutes

Cooking Time: 6 hours

Servings: 5

Ingredients:

1 lb. lean ground beef

3 garlic cloves, crushed

¼ cup of all-purpose flour

1 tbsp. of fresh rosemary, crushed

1 large egg, beaten

½ tsp of salt

3 tbsp. of extra virgin olive oil

For serving:

2 cups of liquid yogurt

1 cup of Greek yogurt

2 tbsp. of fresh parsley

1 garlic clove, crushed

Directions:

1. Mix the ground beef with crushed garlic, rosemary, one egg, and salt in a large bowl. Lightly dampen hands and shape 1 ½

inch balls, transferring them into the greased cooker as you work. Slowly add about ½ cup of water.

2. Cook on low for 4-6 hours. Remove from the cooker and cool completely. Meanwhile, combine liquid yogurt with Greek yogurt, parsley, and crushed garlic. Stir well and drizzle over meatballs.

Nutrition: Calories 477 Proteins 49g Carbohydrates 17.8g Fat 21.4g

Spicy White Peas

Preparation Time: 15 minutes

Cooking Time: 9 hours

Servings: 4

Ingredients:

1 lb. of white peas

4 slices of bacon

1 large onion, finely chopped

1 small chili pepper, finely chopped

2 tbsp. of all-purpose flour

2 tbsp. of butter

1 tbsp. of cayenne pepper

3 bay leaves, dried

1 tsp of salt

½ tsp of freshly ground black pepper

Directions:

1. Melt two tablespoons of butter in a slow cooker. Add chopped onion and stir well. Add bacon, peas, finely chopped chili pepper, bay leaves, salt, and pepper.

2. Gently stir in two tablespoons of flour and add three cups of water. Securely close the lid and cook for 8-9 hours on low or 5 hours on high.

Nutrition: Calories 210 Proteins 4g Carbohydrates 24g Fat 12g 157.

Stuffed Collard Greens

Preparation Time: 15 minutes

Cooking Time: 4 hours

Servings: 5

Ingredients:

1 1/2 lb. of collard greens, steamed

1 lb. lean ground beef

2 small onions, peeled and finely chopped

½ cup long grain rice

2 tbsp. of olive oil

1 tsp of salt

½ tsp of freshly ground black pepper

1 tsp of mint leaves, finely chopped

Directions:

1. Boil a pot of water, then gently put the collard greens. Briefly cook for 2-3 minutes. Drain and gently squeeze the greens and set them aside.

1. Mix the ground beef with the chopped onions, rice, salt, pepper, and mint leaves in a large bowl.

2. Oil the slow cooker with some olive oil. Place leaves on your work surface, vein side up. Use one tablespoon of the meat mixture and place it in the bottom center of each leaf.

3. Fold the sides over and roll up tightly. Tuck in the sides and gently transfer to a slow cooker. Cook on low within ten hours or on high setting for 4 hours.

Nutrition: Calories 156 Proteins 5.2g Carbohydrates 21g Fat 7g

Italian chicken

Serves: 6

Planning: Time: half-hour

Ingredients:

1 carrot, hacked

1/2 lb. mushrooms

8 chicken thighs

1 cup pureed tomatoes

3 cloves garlic, squashed

Preparation:

1. Season the chicken with salt and pepper.

2. Cover and marinate for a half-hour.

3. Press the sauté setting within the Instant Pot.

4. Add 1 tablespoon of ghee.

5. Cook the carrots and mushrooms until delicate.

6. Add the pureed tomatoes and garlic.

7. Add the chicken, tomatoes and olives.

8. Cook and blend well.

9. Seal the pot.

10. Set it to manual.

11. Cook at a high pressing factor for 10 minutes.

12. Release the pressing factor normally.

Serving Suggestion: Garnish with new basil and parsley leaves.

Dietary Information Per Serving: Calories 425, Total Fat 16.9g, Saturated Fat 5.3g, Cholesterol 179mg, Sodium 395mg, Total Carbohydrate 7.5g, Dietary Fibre 2.1g, Total Sugars 4.5g, Protein 58.9g, Potassium 929mg

Lemon garlic chicken

Serves: 6

Arrangement: Time: 1 hour and 20 minutes

Ingredients:

6 chicken bosom filets

3 tablespoons vegetable oil

1 tablespoon juice

3 cloves garlic, squashed and minced

2 teaspoon dried parsley

Preparation:

1. Marinate the chicken bosom filets during a combination of vegetable oil, juice, garlic, parsley, and slightly salt and pepper.

2. Let sit for 1 hour shrouded within the fridge.

3. Press the sauté setting within the Instant Pot.

4 Pour within the oil.

5. Cook the chicken for five minutes for every side or until completely cooked.

Serving Suggestion: Serve with rice or a plate of mixed greens.

Tip: you'll likewise cut the chicken before cooking.

Nourishing Information Per Serving:

Calories 341, Total Fat 17.9g, Saturated Fat 4g, Cholesterol 130mg, Sodium 127mg, Total Carbohydrate 0.7g, Dietary Fibre 0.1g, Total Sugars 0.1g, Protein 42.4g, Potassium 368mg

Chicken with Salsa and Cilantro

Serves: 6

Readiness: Time: half-hour

Ingredients:

1 ½ lb. chicken bosom filets

2 cups salsa Verde

1 teaspoon garlic, minced

1 teaspoon cumin

2 tablespoons new cilantro, chopped

Preparation:

1. Put the chicken bosom filets inside the moment Pot.

2. Pour the salsa, garlic and cumin on top.

3. Seal the pot.

4. Set it to poultry.

5. Release the pressing factor rapidly.

6. Remove the chicken and shred.

7 Put it back to the pot.

8. Mix within the cilantro.

Serving Suggestion: Top with solid avocado shapes and hacked tomatoes.

Tip: you'll likewise utilize garlic powder rather than minced garlic.

Healthful Information Per Serving:

Calories 238, Total Fat 8.7g, Saturated Fat 2.3g, Cholesterol 101mg, Sodium 558mg, Total Carbohydrate 3.8g, Dietary Fibre 0.4g, Total Sugars 1.2g, Protein 34g, Potassium 285mg

Chicken and Rice

Serves: 8

Readiness: Time: 50 minutes

Ingredients:

1 whole chicken, dig smaller pieces.

2 tablespoons dry Greek flavouring

1/2 cups long-grain polished rice

1 cup cleaved parsley

Preparation:

1. Coat the chicken with the flavouring blend.

2. Add 2 cups of water to the moment Pot.

3. Add the chicken inside.

4. Seal the pot.

5. Choose the manual mode.

6. Cook at high pressing factor for a half-hour.

7. Release the pressing factor normally.

8. Lift the chicken and spot it on a preparing sheet.

9 Bake within the stove for five minutes or until the skin is firm.

10. While pausing, strain the stock from the moment Pot to eliminate the chicken build up.

11. Add the rice.

12. Seal the pot.

13. Set it to rice work.

14. Fluff the rice and present it with the chicken.

Healthful Information

Per Serving: Calories 412, Total Fat 11.2g, Saturated Fat 3.1g, Cholesterol 130mg, Sodium 249mg, Total Carbohydrate 29.3g,

Dietary Fibre 0.7g, Total Sugars 0.1g, Protein 45.1g, Potassium 450mg

Chicken shawarma

Serves: 8

Readiness: Time: half-hour

Ingredients:

2 lb. Chicken bosom, dig Strips

1 teaspoon paprika

1 teaspoon ground cumin

1/4 teaspoon granulated garlic

1/2 teaspoon turmeric

1/4 teaspoon ground allspice **Preparation:**

1. Season the chicken with the flavours and somewhat salt and pepper.

2. Pour 1 cup chicken broth into the pot.

3. Seal the pot.

4. Choose a poultry setting.

5. Cook for quarter-hour.

6. Release the pressing factor normally.

Serving Suggestion: Serve with cooked yams.

Healthful Information Per Serving:

Calories 132, Total Fat 3g, Saturated Fat 0g, Cholesterol 73mg, Sodium 58mg, Total Carbohydrate 0.5g, Dietary Fibre 0.2g, Total Sugars 0.1g, Protein 24.2g, Potassium 435mg

Mediterranean chicken

Serves: 6

Readiness: Time: 20 minutes

Ingredients:

2 lb. chicken bosom filet, dig strips

Wine combination (1/4 cup wine blended in with 3 tablespoons red wine) 2 tablespoons light earthy coloured sugar

1/2 teaspoons dried oregano

6 garlic cloves, slashed

Preparation:

1. Pour within the wine combination to the moment Pot.

2. Stir within the remainder of the Ingredients.

3. Toss the chicken to hide equitably.

4. Seal the pot.

5. Set it to a high pressing factor.

6. Cook for 10 minutes.

7 Release the pressing factor normally.

Serving Suggestion: Serve with polished rice.

Wholesome Information

Per Serving: Calories 304, Total Fat 11.3g, Saturated Fat 3.1g, Cholesterol 135mg, Sodium 131mg, Total Carbohydrate 4.2g, Dietary Fibre 0.2g, Total Sugars 3g, Protein 44g, Potassium 390mg

Turkey lasagna

Serves: 4

Readiness: Time: half-hour **Ingredients:**

4 tortillas

1/4 cup salsa

1/2 can frijoles refritos

1/2 cups cooked turkey

1/4 cup cheddar, destroyed

Preparation:

1. Spray a touch container with oil.

2. Spread the frijoles refritos on every tortilla.

3. Place the principal tortilla inside the skillet.

4. Add layers of the turkey, salsa and cheddar.

5. Place another tortilla and rehash the layers.

6. Pour 1 cup of water inside the moment Pot.

7. Place the layers on top of a liner bin.

8. Place the bin inside the moment Pot.

9. Choose the manual setting.

10. Cook at a high pressing factor for 10 minutes.

Serving Suggestion: Top with cleaved parsley.

Tip: you'll likewise add Parmesan cheddar within the cheddar layer.

Dietary Information Per Serving: Calories 335, Total Fat 15.5g, Saturated Fat 8.6g, Cholesterol 79mg, Sodium 849mg, Total Carbohydrate 21.1g, Dietary Fibre 4.5g, Total Sugars 3g, Protein 28.5g, Potassium 561mg

Delectable Beef and Broccoli

Serves: 4

Readiness: Time: 10 minutes

Cooking Time: quarter-hour

Ingredients:

1 and ½ pounds flanks steak, dig slender strips

1 tablespoon vegetable oil

1 tablespoon tamari sauce

1 cup meat stock

1 pound broccoli, florets isolated

Preparation:

1. In a bowl, blend steak strips with oil and tamari, throw and leave to the side for 10 minutes.

2. Set your moment pot on sauté mode, add meat strips, and earthy coloured them for 4 minutes on all sides.

3. Add stock, mix, cover pot again and cook on high for 8 minutes.

4. Add broccoli, mix, cover pot again and cook on high for 4 minutes more.

5. Divide everything among plates and serve.

Sustenance Information Per Serving:

Calories: 312, Protein: 4 g, Fat: 5 g, Carbohydrates: 20 g

Hamburger corn chili:

Serves: 8

Readiness: Time: 8-10 minutes

Cooking Time: half-hour

Ingredients: 2 little onions, cleaved (finely)

¼ cup canned corn

1 tablespoon oil

10 ounces lean ground meat

2 small stew peppers, diced

Preparation:

1. Take your moment pot and spot over dry kitchen surface; open its top and switch it on.

2. Press. "SAUTE".

3. In its Cooking pot, add and heat the oil.

4. Add the onions, stew pepper, and hamburger; cook for 2-3 minutes until turn clear and relaxed.

5. Add the three cups of water within the Cooking pot; join in blending well.

6. Close its top cover and make sure that its valve it shut to abstain from spilling.

7. Press "MEAT/STEW". Change the clock to twenty minutes.

8. Press will gradually develop; let the extra Ingredients to cook until the clock shows zero.

9. Press "Drop". Presently press "NPR" for characteristic delivery pressure. Moment pot will, step by step, deliver pressure for around 8-10 minutes.

10. Open the highest cover; move the cooked formula to serve plates.

11. Serve the formula warm.

Nourishment Information Per Serving:

Calories: 94, Protein: 7 g, Fat: 5 g, Carbohydrates: 2 g

Balsamic beef dish

Serves: 8

Readiness: Time: 5 minutes

Cooking Time: 55 minutes

Ingredients: 3 pounds toss broil

3 cloves garlic, meagrely cut

1 tablespoon oil

1 teaspoon enhanced vinegar

½ teaspoon pepper

½ teaspoon rosemary

1 tablespoon margarine

½ teaspoon thyme

¼ cup balsamic vinegar

1 cup hamburger stock

Planning:

1. Cut cuts within the meal and stuff garlic cuts all finished.

2. Take a bowl and add enhanced vinegar, rosemary, pepper, thyme, and rub the mixture over the dish.

3. Set your pot to sauté mode and add oil, permit the oil to warm up.

4. Add meal and earthy coloured the 2 sides (5 minutes each side).

5. Take the meal out and keep it as an afterthought.

6. Add spread, stock, balsamic vinegar and deglaze the pot.

7. Transfer the meal back and lock up the duvet, cook on HIGH pressing factor for 40 minutes.

8. Perform a brisk delivery.

9. Remove the highest and serve!

Nourishment Information Per Serving: Calories: 393, Protein: 37 g, Fat: 15 g, Carbohydrates: 25 g

Mediterranean Pork and Orzo

Preparation Time: 15 minutes

Cooking Time: 20 minutes

Servings: 1

Ingredients:

1-1/2 pounds pork tenderloin

One teaspoon coarsely ground pepper

One package (6 ounces) of fresh baby spinach

1 cup grape tomatoes, halved

3/4 cup crumbled feta cheese

Two tablespoons olive oil

3 quarts water

1-1/4 cups uncooked orzo pasta

1/4 teaspoon salt

Directions:

Ø Pork should be rubbed with pepper and chopped into 1-inch chunks. Heat the oil in a large nonstick skillet over medium heat. Cook and stir until the pork is no longer pink, 8-10 minutes.

Ø Meanwhile, bring water to a boil in a Dutch oven. Cook, uncovered, for 8 minutes after adding orzo and salt. Cook until the orzo is cooked, and the spinach is wilted, 45-60 seconds more. Drain.

Ø Heat through the tomatoes with the meat. Stir in the orzo-cheese mixture.

Ground Beef Sweet Potato Curry

Preparation Time: 15 minutes

Cooking Time: 20 minutes

Servings: 1

Ingredients:

Two sweet potatoes (peeled and cut in half)

Two onions (peeled and quartered)

1 1/2 teaspoons coriander

Two teaspoons paprika

1/2 teaspoon cayenne (to taste)

1 1/4 teaspoons salt

pepper (to taste)

1 cup frozen peas

Four tomatoes

1/4-pound ground beef

27 ounces unsweetened coconut milk (full fat)

Three tablespoons minced garlic

Four teaspoons Garam Masala

Directions:

Ø Hand-dice the sweet potatoes, onion, and tomatoes, or use the KitchenAid® Pro Line® Series 16-Cup Food Processor with Commercial-Style Dicing.

Ø Heat several tablespoons of olive oil in a large sauté pan and add the diced veggies. Cook for 10 minutes on high, often turning to prevent scorching until veggies begin to soften.

Ø Cook until the ground beef and garlic are browned in the center of the pan, about 5 minutes.

Ø Cook for 5 minutes on medium heat with coconut milk and spices. Season with salt and pepper to taste. Can be kept on the lowest heat setting on the stove until ready to serve (up to 1 hour).

Ø Add frozen peas five minutes before serving. Serve with rice and naan bread (or roti).

Pasta with Ground Beef

Preparation Time: 15 minutes

Cooking Time: 20 minutes

Servings: 1

Ingredients:

One clove garlic

One carrot

1 3/4 cups water

One teaspoon chicken bouillon (powdered)

One tablespoon Worcestershire sauce

1 cup whole wheat short pasta

salt

Four mushrooms

1/4 onion

One tablespoon olive oil

200 grams ground beef

ground black pepper

Two tablespoons low-fat sour cream

Two tablespoons fresh parsley (chopped)

Directions:

Ø Chop the garlic, carrot, mushrooms, and onion finely.

Ø Warm the oil in a big saucepan over low heat. Mix in the ground beef. When the color changes, add the veggies. 5 minutes in the oven

Ø Season with salt and pepper after adding the water, bouillon powder, Worcestershire sauce, and pasta.

Ø Cook, covered, for 8 to 10 minutes, or until the pasta is tender.

Ø Uncover the pot and cook until the water has totally evaporated. Turn off the heat and mix in the cream. Serve immediately with a sprinkle of parsley on top. If preferred, top with Parmesan cheese.

Hearty Ground Beef Pizza

Preparation Time: 15 minutes

Cooking Time: 20 minutes

Servings: 1

Ingredients:

1/2-pound ground beef

1/4 cup sliced green onions

1 cup shredded mozzarella cheese

3/4 cup ragu pizza quick sauce

12 prebaked pizza crusts (prebaked)

One red bell pepper, sliced (small)

Directions:

Ø Preheat the oven to 450 degrees.

Ø Brown ground beef in a 12-inch nonstick pan over medium-high heat; drain. Season with salt and pepper to taste. Spread the sauce evenly over the pizza dough, then top with the ground beef, red pepper, onions, and cheese. Bake for 12 minutes or until the cheese has melted.

Black-Eyed Pea and Ground Beef Chili

Preparation Time: 15 minutes

Cooking Time: 20 minutes

Servings: 1

Ingredients:

100 grams black-eyed peas

One can peel tomatoes (in juice)

Three tablespoons parsley

Three teaspoons spice blend (Texas)

One red pepper

Two onions

Two tablespoons olive oil

400 grams ground beef

salt (to taste)

Directions:

Ø Rinse peas in cold water and cook for 1 hour and 15 minutes in water.

Ø Wash and chop the pepper into tiny bits.

Ø The onion should be peeled and sliced.

Greek Burgers

Preparation Time: 15 minutes

Cooking Time: 20 minutes

Servings: 1

Ingredients:

Five pita bread (sections)

1/4 cup milk

250 grams ground beef

lettuce leaves

1/2 red onion (peeled and sliced)

1/2 cup feta cheese (diced)

1 cup plain yogurt

One tablespoon Dijon mustard

1/2 teaspoon honey

1/2 cup cucumber (seeded and diced)

One tablespoon mint (minced)

One garlic clove (peeled and minced)

salt

250 grams ground pork

Two tablespoons mint (minced)

1/2 lemon

Two tablespoons onion (minced)

One garlic clove (peeled and minced)

1/2 teaspoon dried oregano

One tomato (sliced)

Directions:

Ø Each pita should be cut in half so that 1/5 of it is removed. Slices should be minced and marinated in milk for 10 minutes. The bread should be strained.

Ø In a large mixing bowl, combine the strained bread, meat, pork, mint, lemon juice, onion, garlic, oregano, and a pinch of salt and pepper. Using your hands, shape the burgers.

Ø Grill the burgers in a pan coated with cooking spray over medium heat until golden brown on both sides.

Ø Combine the plain yogurt, Dijon mustard, honey, mint, garlic, and salt and black pepper in a small bowl.

Ø Cut open the pita bread, sprinkle the dressing on top, then top with the lettuce, meat, tomato, red onion, and Feta cheese. Serve with more dressing on top.

Mediterranean Pork Tenderloin Crostini

Preparation Time: 15 minutes

Cooking Time: 20 minutes

Servings: 1

Ingredients:

6 ounces roasted red peppers (well-drained)

Three tablespoons finely chopped fresh basil

12 slices baguette (toasted)

4 ounces garlic-and-herbs chèvre goat cheese (soft) chopped fresh thyme (for garnish, optional)

1-ounce shredded Parmesan cheese (1/4 cup)

One pork tenderloin (1- to 1 ½-pound)

Two tablespoons extra virgin olive oil

Two tablespoons aged balsamic vinegar 1/2 teaspoon coarse ground black pepper

1/2 teaspoon garlic salt

nonstick cooking spray

Directions:

Ø Heat the oven to 425°F.

Ø Using a paper towel, pat dries the roasted peppers; coarsely slice the red peppers to form 34 cups. Combine the chopped red peppers, basil, and Parmesan cheese in a small mixing dish. Set aside the mixture.

Ø Using paper towels, pat the pork tenderloin dry. Trim the silver skin and connective tissue from the pork tenderloin using a keen, thin knife. Make a longitudinal cut across the tenderloin's middle. Cut to the opposite side, but not through it. Open the meat so that it is flat. Distribute the red pepper mixture equally over half of the tenderloin. Fold the other half of the pork over to create the tenderloin's original shape. Tie the ends together with kitchen string at 1- to 112-inch intervals.

Ø In a separate small bowl, whisk together the olive oil, balsamic vinegar, black pepper, and garlic salt; put aside.

Ø The tenderloin should be rubbed with the balsamic mixture. Spray a shallow roasting pan rack lightly with nonstick spray. Place the tenderloin on the prepared rack in the pan.

Ø Cook, uncovered, for 20 to 35 minutes, or until an instant-read thermometer placed near the middle and without touching the filling registers 145°F. Cool the tenderloin for 30 minutes on a chopping board. Wrap the pork in plastic wrap and place it in the refrigerator for at least 4 hours or overnight.

Ø To serve, spread goat cheese on baguette toasts. Remove the threads from the pork tenderloin and chop them into 3/8-inch pieces. Spray the rack in a shallow roasting pan lightly with nonstick spray. Arrange the pieces on top of the goat cheese. If desired, garnish with thyme.

Herb-Crusted Mediterranean Pork Tenderloin

Preparation Time: 15 minutes

Cooking Time: 20 minutes

Servings: 1

Ingredients:

1 pound pork tenderloin

Three tablespoons olive tapenade (refrigerated mixed) 1-ounce feta cheese (finely crumbled, about three tablespoons) One tablespoon olive oil

Two teaspoons dried oregano

3/4 teaspoon lemon pepper

Directions:

Ø Place the pork on a big sheet of plastic wrap. The tenderloin should be rubbed with oil, then sprinkled with oregano and lemon pepper equally over the top. Wrap securely with plastic wrap and place in the refrigerator for 2 hours or overnight.

Ø Make a medium-hot fire in the grill. Unwrap the meat. Make a longitudinal cut across the tenderloin's middle. Cut to the opposite side, but not through it. Open the meat so that it is flat. Half of the tenderloin should be spread with olive tapénade. Garnish with cheese. Fold the other half of the meat over to create the tenderloin's original shape. Tie rope at 1 1/2 to 2-inch intervals to close.

Ø Grill tenderloin over the direct fire for 20 minutes, or until internal temperature reaches 145°F*, rotating tenderloin halfway through cooking. Place the tenderloin on a chopping board. Cover loosely with foil and set aside for 5-10 minutes. Remove the thread and cut the pieces into 1/4-inch-thick slices to serve.

Mediterranean Pork with Olives

Preparation Time: 15 minutes

Cooking Time: 20 minutes

Servings: 1

Ingredients:

One tablespoon olive oil

Pasta Sauce (1 lb. 8 oz.)

1/2 cup ripe olives (sliced, pitted)

One pinch of ground cinnamon (optional)

Six bone-in pork chops (or boneless pork chops, 3/4 inch thick)
One onion (large, sliced)

Two cloves' garlic (finely chopped)

1/4 cup dry white wine

Directions:

Ø Brown the chops in a 12-inch pan over medium-high heat; remove and set aside.

Ø In the same skillet, cook onion and garlic over medium heat, turning periodically until the onion is soft. Bring wine to a boil over high heat, scraping brown pieces from the bottom of the skillet. Return the meat to the skillet and combine it with the Pasta Sauce and the additional ingredients.

Ø Cook, covered, for 20 minutes, or until the meat is cooked through. If preferred, serve over hot cooked rice and sprinkle with fresh rosemary and extra olives.

Greek Beef Pitas

Preparation Time: 15 minutes

Cooking Time: 20 minutes

Servings: 1

Ingredients:

1-pound lean ground beef (90% lean)

One small onion, chopped

1/2 cup chopped peeled cucumber

One teaspoon dill weed

Four whole pita bread, warmed

Three garlic cloves, minced

One teaspoon dried oregano

3/4 teaspoon salt, divided

1 cup reduced fat plain Greek yogurt

One medium tomato, chopped

Directions:

Ø Cook beef, onion, and garlic in a large pan over medium heat for 8-10

minutes, or until the meat is no longer pink and veggies are soft, breaking steak into crumbles; drain. Add the oregano and 1/2 teaspoon salt and mix well.

Ø Combine the yogurt, tomato, cucumber, dill, and the remaining ¼ teaspoon salt in a small mixing bowl. Top each pita with 3/4 cup beef mixture and three tablespoons yogurt sauce. Top with more tomatoes and cucumber, if preferred. Serve with any leftover yogurt sauce.

Quinoa, Chicken & Broccoli Salad

Preparation Time: 15 minutes

Cooking Time: 20 minutes

Servings: 1

Ingredients:

1 (8 ounces) boneless, skinless chicken breast, trimmed Four tablespoons extra-virgin olive oil, divided 8 ounces broccoli with stems (about one medium head) ¼ cup red-wine vinegar

One tablespoon Dijon mustard

2 cups arugula

¾ cup chopped walnuts, toasted

½ cup dried cranberries

½ cup chopped fresh mint

⅛ teaspoon salt plus 1/4 teaspoon, divided

Two small lemons, thinly sliced and seeded

1 cup low-sodium chicken broth

½ cup quinoa

Directions:

Ø Preheat the oven to 425°F.

Ø Place the chicken on one side of a baking sheet with a rim. Drizzle one tablespoon oil over the top and season with 1/8 teaspoon salt. Ten minutes in the oven on the other side of the baking sheet, arrange the lemon slices. 7 to 9 minutes more, or until an instant-read thermometer inserted into the thickest part of the chicken registers 160°F, the lemons are browned.

Ø Meanwhile, bring broth and quinoa to a boil in a small saucepan. Reduce the heat to maintain a simmer, cover, and cook for 15 minutes until the liquid is absorbed. Remove from the heat and set aside for 10 minutes, covered.

Ø Remove the broccoli florets from the stalks. Trim, peel, and finely slice the stems, then cut the florets into bite-sized pieces.

Ø Half of the lemon segments should be chopped. In a large mixing bowl, combine the vinegar, mustard, and the remaining three tablespoons of oil, as well as 1/4 teaspoon salt.

Ø Chicken should be shredded. Toss together the chicken, remaining lemon slices, broccoli, quinoa, arugula, walnuts, cranberries, and mint with the dressing.

Chicken & Farro Herb Salad

Preparation Time: 15 minutes

Cooking Time: 20 minutes

Servings: 1

Ingredients:

red-Wine Vinaigrette

⅓ cup red-wine vinegar

1 ½ tablespoon Dijon mustard

3 cups water

1 cup farro

1 ½ pound boneless, skinless chicken breast, trimmed ½ teaspoon kosher salt

¼ teaspoon ground pepper

One fennel bulb, cored and chopped

1 cup diced carrot

One small clove of garlic, minced

¾ teaspoon kosher salt

½ teaspoon ground pepper

½ cup extra-virgin olive oil

1 cup chopped seeded English cucumber

½ cup finely chopped red onion

¼ cup chopped flat-leaf parsley

¼ cup fresh basil, very thinly sliced

¼ cup fresh mint, very thinly sliced

2 cups arugula, tough stems removed, coarsely chopped ¼ cup oil-cured black olives, sliced

Directions:

Ø To make the vinaigrette: In a medium mixing bowl, combine the vinegar, mustard, garlic, 3/4 teaspoon salt, and 1/2 teaspoon pepper. Whisk in the oil.

Ø Salad

Preparation: In a medium saucepan, bring water to a boil. Reduce the heat to low, cover, and cook until the farro is barely cooked for 15 to 25 minutes. Drain the farro and place it in a large mixing bowl.

Ø Toss the heated farro with 1/3 cup of the vinaigrette and let it chill.

Ø Preheat the grill to medium-high heat.

Ø Season the chicken with salt and pepper to taste. Lubricate the grill rack. Grill the chicken, turning once or twice, for 12 to 16 minutes, or until cooked through. Allow it cool for 5 minutes before slicing.

Ø Farro, fennel, carrot, cucumber, onion, parsley, basil, mint, and 1/3 cup vinaigrette

Ø Stir the arugula into the farro mixture just before serving. Serve with the remaining vinaigrette poured over the chicken and olives.

Green Salad with Pita Bread & Hummus
Preparation Time: 15 minutes

Cooking Time: 20 minutes

Servings: 1

Ingredients:

2 cups mixed salad greens

½ cup sliced cucumber

Two tablespoons grated carrot

1 6 1/2-inch whole-wheat pita bread, toasted

¼ cup hummus

1 ½ teaspoon extra-virgin olive oil

1 ½ teaspoon balsamic vinegar

Pinch of salt

Pinch of ground pepper

Directions:

Ø On a big platter, arrange the greens, cucumber, and carrot. Drizzle with oil and vinegar to taste—season with salt and pepper to taste. Serve with pita bread and hummus on the side.

Chicken Souvlaki Kebabs with Mediterranean Couscous

Preparation Time: 15 minutes

Cooking Time: 20 minutes

Servings: 1

Ingredients:

Chicken Souvlaki Kabobs

1-pound skinless, boneless chicken breast halves 1 cup sliced fennel (reserve leaves, if desired) ⅓ cup dry white wine

Mediterranean Couscous

One teaspoon olive oil

½ cup Israeli (large pearl) couscous

1 cup water

½ cup snipped dried tomatoes (not oil-packed)

¾ cup chopped red sweet pepper

½ cup chopped cucumber

½ cup chopped red onion

¼ cup lemon juice

Three tablespoons canola oil

Four cloves' garlic, minced

Two teaspoons dried oregano, crushed

½ teaspoon salt

¼ teaspoon black pepper

Lemon wedges

⅓ cup plain fat-free Greek yogurt

¼ cup thinly sliced fresh basil leaves

¼ cup snipped fresh parsley

One tablespoon lemon juice

¼ teaspoon salt

¼ teaspoon black pepper

Directions:

Ø Combine the chicken and sliced fennel in a resealable plastic bag in a shallow dish to make the kabobs. In a small mixing bowl, combine the white wine, lemon juice, oil, garlic, oregano, salt, and pepper for the marinade. Set aside a quarter cup of the marinade.

Ø Pour the rest of the marinade over the chicken mixture. Close bag and flip to coat chicken mixture. Refrigerate for 1 1/2 hours, turning the bag once.

Ø Meanwhile, soak eight 10- to 12-inch wooden skewers in water for 30 minutes if used. Drain the chicken, reserving the marinade and fennel. Thread chicken onto skewers accordion-style.

Ø Grill the chicken skewers, covered, for 6 to 8 minutes, or until the chicken is no longer pink, flipping once. Remove off the grill and brush with the 1/4 cup marinade that has been set aside.

Ø Make the couscous: 1 teaspoon olive oil, heated in a small saucepan over medium heat 1 cup Israeli (big pearl) couscous Cook and stir for 4 minutes, or until the mixture is light brown. One cup of water Bring to a boil, then turn off the heat. Cook, covered, for 10 minutes, or until the couscous is soft and the liquid has been absorbed; add 1/2 cup chopped dried tomatoes (not oil-packed) in the final 5 minutes; cool. Place the couscous in a large mixing basin. 1/3 cup plain fat-free Greek yogurt, 1/4 cup each thinly sliced fresh basil leaves and snipped fresh parsley, one tablespoon lemon juice, and 1/4 teaspoon each salt and black pepper

Ø Kabobs should be served with couscous, lemon wedges, and, if preferred, saved fennel leaves.

Slow-Cooker Chicken Cacciatore with Polenta

Preparation Time: 15 minutes

Cooking Time: 20 minutes

Servings: 1

Ingredients:

Two teaspoons extra-virgin olive oil

2 cups chopped red bell peppers

2 cups chopped yellow onion

8 ounces cremini mushrooms, halved

½ teaspoon kosher salt, divided

½ cup red wine

4 pounds bone-in, skinless chicken thighs, trimmed 1 (28 ounces) can fire-roasted diced tomatoes

1 cup unsalted chicken broth

¼ cup drained capers

¼ cup pitted Kalamata olives

3 cups water

One ⅓ cups uncooked instant polenta

¼ cup grated Parmesan cheese

¼ cup torn fresh basil

Three tablespoons all-purpose flour

One tablespoon tomato paste

Three tablespoons minced garlic

¼ cup chopped fresh oregano

½ teaspoon crushed red pepper

Directions:

Ø In a large skillet over medium-high heat, heat the oil. Cook, frequently stirring, until the bell peppers, onion, and mushrooms begin to brown, approximately 8 minutes. Cook, stirring regularly, until the flour, tomato paste, garlic, oregano, and crushed red pepper are aromatic, approximately 1 minute. Cook for 30 seconds, stirring and scraping up any browned pieces.

Ø Fill a 6-quart slow cooker halfway with the ingredients. Combine the chicken, tomatoes, broth, and capers in a mixing bowl. Cook on Low for 8 hours, covered.

Ø Transfer the chicken to a clean chopping board and set aside for 5 minutes to cool. Return the meat to the slow cooker after removing the bones. Combine the olives and the remaining 1/4 teaspoon salt in a mixing bowl. Keep warm by covering.

Ø Meanwhile, in a medium saucepan over medium-high heat, bring water to a boil. Cook, often stirring, until the polenta thickens, approximately 3 minutes. Remove from the heat and whisk in the Parmesan cheese. Serve the chicken and sauce on top of the polenta, garnished with basil.

Mediterranean Chicken with Orzo Salad

Preparation Time: 15 minutes

Cooking Time: 20 minutes

Servings: 1

Ingredients:

Two skinless, boneless chicken breasts (8 ounces each), halved Three tablespoons extra-virgin olive oil, divided One teaspoon lemon zest

¼ cup crumbled feta cheese

Two tablespoons chopped Kalamata olives

Two tablespoons lemon juice

One clove garlic, grated

Two teaspoons chopped fresh oregano

½ teaspoon salt, divided

½ teaspoon ground pepper, divided

¾ cup whole-wheat orzo

2 cups thinly sliced baby spinach

1 cup chopped cucumber

1 cup chopped tomato

¼ cup chopped red onion

Directions:

Ø Preheat the oven to 425°F.

Ø Brush the chicken with one tablespoon oil and season with ¼ teaspoon salt and pepper. Put it in a baking dish. Bake for 25 to 30

minutes, or until an instant-read thermometer inserted into the thickest section registers 165 degrees F.

Ø Meanwhile, in a medium saucepan over high heat, bring a quart of water to a boil. Cook for 8 minutes after adding the orzo. Cook for 1 minute more after adding the spinach. Rinse with cold water after draining. Drain well and transfer to a large mixing bowl. Cucumber, tomato, onion, feta, and olives are optional. To blend, stir everything together.

Ø Combine the remaining two tablespoons of oil, lemon juice, garlic, oregano, and 1/4 teaspoon salt and pepper in a separate dish. The dressing should be mixed into the orzo mixture except for one tablespoon. Serve the chicken with the leftover dressing on top of the salad.

Sheet-Pan Mediterranean Chicken, Brussels Sprouts & Gnocchi

Preparation Time: 15 minutes

Cooking Time: 20 minutes

Servings: 1

Ingredients:

Four tablespoons extra-virgin olive oil, divided Two tablespoons chopped fresh oregano, divided

Two large cloves of garlic, minced, divided

½ teaspoon ground pepper, divided Four boneless, skinless chicken thighs, trimmed

1 cup halved cherry tomatoes

One tablespoon red-wine vinegar

¼ teaspoon salt, divided

1 pound Brussels sprouts, trimmed and quartered

1 (16 ounces) package shelf-stable gnocchi

1 cup sliced red onion

Directions:

Ø Preheat the oven to 450°F.

Ø In a large mixing bowl, combine two tablespoons of oil, one tablespoon oregano, half the garlic, 1/4 teaspoon pepper, and 1/8 teaspoon salt. Toss in the Brussels sprouts, gnocchi, and onion to coat. Spread the mixture on a broad-rimmed baking sheet.

Ø In a large mixing bowl, combine one tablespoon oil, the remaining one tablespoon oregano, the remaining garlic, 1/4 teaspoon pepper, and 1/8 teaspoon salt. Toss in the chicken to coat. Place the chicken in the center of the veggie mixture. 10 minutes in the oven

Ø Remove from the oven and whisk in the tomatoes to mix. Continue roasting for another 10 minutes, or until the Brussels sprouts are soft and the chicken is cooked through. Combine the vegetable mixture with the vinegar and the remaining one tablespoon oil.

Chicken & Spinach Soup with Fresh Pesto
Preparation Time: 15 minutes

Cooking Time: 20 minutes

Servings: 1

Ingredients:

Two teaspoons plus one tablespoon extra-virgin olive oil, divided ½ cup carrot or diced red bell pepper

One large boneless, skinless chicken breast (about 8 ounces), cut into quarters

Freshly ground pepper to taste

One large clove of garlic, minced

5 cups reduced-sodium chicken broth

1 ½ teaspoons dried marjoram

6 ounces baby spinach, coarsely chopped One 15-ounce can of cannellini beans or great northern beans, rinsed ¼ cup grated Parmesan cheese

⅓ cup lightly packed fresh basil leaves

Directions:

Ø In a large pot or Dutch oven, heat two tablespoons of oil over medium-high heat. Cook, rotate the chicken, and stir regularly until the chicken brown for 3 to 4 minutes. Cook for 1 minute further, stirring constantly, after adding the garlic. Bring broth and marjoram to a boil over high heat. Reduce the heat to low and cook, stirring regularly, for 5 minutes, or until the chicken is cooked through.

Ø Transfer the chicken pieces to a clean chopping board to cool using a slotted spoon. Bring the spinach and beans to a mild boil in the saucepan. Cook for 5 minutes to allow the flavors to mix.

Ø Combine the remaining tablespoon oil, Parmesan, and basil (a mini processor works well). Add a little water as needed and process until coarse paste forms, scraping down the sides as needed.

Ø Chicken should be cut into bite-size pieces. Incorporate the chicken and pesto into the saucepan. Season with pepper to taste. Heat until it is hot. If desired, garnish with croutons.

Greek Kale Salad with Quinoa & Chicken

Preparation Time: 15 minutes

Cooking Time: 20 minutes

Servings: 1

Ingredients:

4 cups chopped kale

¼ cup Greek salad dressing (see Tip)

1-ounce crumbled feta cheese

1 ½ cups shredded cooked chicken

1 cup cooked quinoa

¼ cup sliced jarred roasted red peppers

Directions:

Ø Combine the greens, chicken, quinoa, and roasted peppers in a large mixing bowl. Toss in the dressing to coat. If preferred, top with feta.

Hasselback Caprese Chicken

Preparation Time: 15 minutes

Cooking Time: 20 minutes

Servings: 1

Ingredients:

Two boneless, skinless chicken breasts (8 ounces each) 8 cups broccoli florets

Two tablespoons extra-virgin olive oil

½ teaspoon salt, divided

½ teaspoon ground pepper, divided

One medium tomato, sliced

3 ounces fresh mozzarella, halved and sliced

¼ cup prepared pesto

Directions:

Ø Preheat the oven to 375°F. I am cooking spray on a big, rimmed baking sheet.

Ø Make 1/2-inch crosswise slices and both chicken breasts, to the bottom but not through—Season the chicken with 1/4 teaspoon salt and ¼ teaspoon pepper. Alternately stuff the cuts with tomato and mozzarella slices. Brush on pesto. Place the chicken on one side of the baking sheet that has been prepped.

Ø Combine broccoli, oil, and the remaining 1/4 teaspoon salt and pepper in a large mixing bowl. If you have any leftover tomato slices, toss them in. Place the broccoli mixture on the baking sheet's empty side.

Ø Bake for 25 minutes, or until the chicken is no longer pink in the center and the broccoli is soft. Serve each breast half-cut with broccoli.

Chicken With Halloumi Cheese

Servings:4

Cooking Time:40 Minutes

Ingredients:

2 tbsp butter

1 cup Halloumi cheese, cubed

Salt and black pepper to taste

1 hard-boiled egg yolk

½ cup olive oil

6 black olives, halved

1 tbsp fresh cilantro, chopped

1 tbsp balsamic vinegar

1 tbsp garlic, finely minced

1 tbsp fresh lemon juice

1 ½ lb chicken wings

Directions:

1. Melt the butter in a saucepan over medium heat. Sear the chicken wings for 5 minutes per side. Season with salt and pepper to taste. Place the chicken wings on a parchment-lined baking pan. Mash the egg yolk with a fork and mix in the garlic, lemon juice, balsamic vinegar, olive oil, and salt until creamy, uniform, and smooth.

2. Preheat oven to 380° F. Spread the egg mixture over the chicken. Bake for 15-20 minutes. Top with the cheese and bake

an additional 5 minutes until hot and bubbly. Scatter cilantro and olives on top of the chicken wings. Serve.

Nutrition Info:

Per Serving: Calories: 560;Fat: 48g;Protein: 41g;Carbs: 2g.

Carrot, Potato & Chicken Bake

Servings:4

Cooking Time:60 Minutes

Ingredients:

2 tbsp olive oil

1 lb chicken breasts, cubed

1 carrot, chopped

2 garlic cloves, minced

Salt and black pepper to taste

2 tsp thyme, dried

1 baby potatoes, halved

1 onion, sliced

¾ cup chicken stock

2 tbsp basil, chopped

Directions:

1. Preheat the oven to 380° F. Grease a baking dish with oil. Put carrot, potatoes, chicken, garlic, salt, pepper, thyme, onion, stock, and basil in the dish and bake for 50 minutes. Serve.

Nutrition Info: Per Serving: Calories: 290;Fat: 10g;Protein: 15g;Carbs: 23g.

Pork Tenderloin With Caraway Seeds

Servings:4

Cooking Time:30 Minutes

Ingredients:

2 tbsp olive oil

1 lb pork tenderloin, sliced

Salt and black pepper to taste

3 tbsp ground caraway seeds

1/3 cup half-and-half

½ cup dill, chopped

Directions:

1. Warm the olive oil in a skillet over medium heat and sear pork for 8 minutes on all sides. Stir in salt, pepper, ground caraway seeds, half-and-half, and dill and bring to a boil. Cook for another 12 minutes. Serve warm.

Nutrition Info: Per Serving: Calories: 330;Fat: 15g;Protein: 18g;Carbs: 15g.

Spicy Beef Zoodles

Servings:4

Cooking Time:20 Minutes

Ingredients:

2 tbsp olive oil

1 lb beef steaks, sliced

2 zucchinis, spiralized

½ cup sweet chili sauce

1 cup carrot, grated

3 tbsp water

Salt and black pepper to taste

Directions:

1. Warm the olive oil in a skillet over medium heat and brown beef steaks for 8 minutes on both side; reserve and cover with foil to keep warm. Stir zucchini noodles, chili sauce, carrot, water, salt, and pepper and cook for an additional 3-4 minutes. Remove the foil from the steaks and pour the zucchini mix over to serve.

Nutrition Info: Per Serving: Calories: 360;Fat: 12g;Protein: 37g;Carbs: 26g.

Spiced Beef Meatballs

Servings:4

Cooking Time:25 Minutes

Ingredients:

¼ cup fresh mozzarella cheese, crumbled

1 lb ground beef

¼ cup panko breadcrumbs

Salt and black pepper to taste

1 red onion, grated

2 tbsp parsley, chopped

2 garlic cloves, minced

1 lemon, juiced and zested

1 egg

½ tsp ground cumin

½ tsp ground coriander

¼ tsp cinnamon powder

Directions:

1. Preheat oven to 390° F. Line a baking sheet with parchment paper. Combine beef, breadcrumbs, salt, pepper, onion, parsley, garlic, lemon juice, lemon zest, egg, cumin, coriander, cinnamon powder, and fresh mozzarella cheese in a bowl and form balls out of the mixture. Place meatballs on the sheet and bake for 15 minutes. Serve warm.

Nutrition Info:

Per Serving: Calories: 310;Fat: 16g;Protein: 36g;Carbs: 23g.

Cranberry Turkey Bake

Servings:4

Cooking Time:40 Minutes

Ingredients:

2 tbsp canola oil

1 turkey breast, sliced

1 cup chicken stock

½ cup cranberry sauce

½ cup orange juice

1 tsp mustard powder

1 onion, chopped

Salt and black pepper to taste

Directions:

1. Warm canola oil in a saucepan over medium heat. Cook onion for 3 minutes. Put in turkey and cook for another 5 minutes, turning once. Season with mustard powder, salt, and pepper. Pour in the cranberry sauce, chicken stock, and orange juice and bring to a boil; simmer for 20 minutes.

Nutrition Info: Per Serving: Calories: 390;Fat: 14g;Protein: 19g;Carbs: 28g.

Lamb Kofta (spiced Meatballs)

Servings:2

Cooking Time: 30 Minutes

Ingredients:

¼ cup walnuts

1 garlic clove

½ small onion

1 roasted piquillo pepper

2 tablespoons fresh mint

2 tablespoons fresh parsley

¼ teaspoon cumin

¼ teaspoon allspice

¼ teaspoon salt

Pinch cayenne pepper

8 ounces lean ground lamb

Directions:

1. Preheat the oven to 350ºF. Line a baking sheet with aluminum foil.

2. In a food processor, combine the walnuts, garlic, onion, roasted pepper, mint, parsley, cumin, allspice, salt, and cayenne pepper. Pulse about 10 times to combine everything.

3. Transfer the spice mixture to a large bowl and add the ground lamb.

With your hands or a spatula, mix the spices into the lamb.

4. Roll the lamb into 1½-inch balls (about the size of golf balls).

5. Arrange the meatballs on the prepared baking sheet and bake for 30 minutes, or until cooked to an internal temperature of 165ºF.

Nutrition Info: Per Serving: Calories: 409;Fat: 22.9g;Protein: 22.0g;Carbs: 7.1g.

Easy Grilled Pork Chops
Servings:4

Cooking Time: 10 Minutes

Ingredients:

¼ cup extra-virgin olive oil

2 tablespoons fresh thyme leaves

1 teaspoon smoked paprika

1 teaspoon salt

4 pork loin chops, ½-inch-thick

Directions:

1. In a small bowl, mix together the olive oil, thyme, paprika, and salt.

2. Put the pork chops in a plastic zip-top bag or a bowl and coat them with the spice mix. Let them marinate for 15 minutes.

3. Preheat the grill to high heat. Cook the pork chops for 4 minutes on each side until cooked through.

Nutrition Info: Per Serving: Calories: 282;Fat: 23.0g;Protein: 21.0g;Carbs: 1.0g.

Baked Beef With Kale Slaw & Bell Peppers

Servings:4

Cooking Time:35 Minutes

Ingredients:

2 tsp olive oil

1 lb skirt steak

4 cups kale slaw

1 tbsp garlic powder

Salt and black pepper to taste

1 small red onion, sliced

10 sundried tomatoes, halved

½ red bell pepper, sliced

Directions:

1. Preheat the broiler. Brush steak with olive oil, salt, garlic powder, and pepper and place under the broiler for 10 minutes, turning once. Remove to a cutting board and let rest for 10 minutes, then cut the steak diagonally.

2. In the meantime, place sun-dried tomatoes, kale slaw, onion, and bell pepper in a bowl and mix to combine. Transfer to a serving plate and top with steak slices to serve.

Nutrition Info: Per Serving: Calories: 359;Fat: 16g;Protein: 38g;Carbs: 22g.

FISH AND SEAFOOD RECIPES

Speedy Tilapia with Red Onion and Avocado

Preparation Time: 10 minutes

Cooking Time: 5 minutes

Servings: 4

Ingredients:

1 tablespoon extra-virgin olive oil

1 tablespoon freshly squeezed orange juice

¼ teaspoon kosher or sea salt

4 (4-ounce) tilapia fillets, more oblong than square, skin-on or skinned ¼ cup chopped red onion

1 avocado

Directions:

1. In a 9-inch glass pie dish, combine the oil, orange juice, and salt.

2. Work on the fillet simultaneously, situate each in the pie dish, and coat on all sides.

3. Form the fillets in a wagon-wheel formation. Place each fillet with 1 tablespoon of onion, then fold the end of the fillet that's hanging over the edge in half over the onion.

4. Once done, you should have 4 folded-over fillets with the fold against the outer edge of the dish and the ends all in the center.

5. Wrap the dish with plastic leaves a small part open at the edge to vent the steam. Cook on high for about 3 minutes in the microwave.

6. When done, it should separate into flakes (chunks) when pressed gently with a fork. Garnish the fillets with the avocado and serve.

Nutrition Calories 200 Fat 3g Carbs 4g Protein 22g

Grilled Fish on Lemons

Preparation Time: 10 minutes

Cooking Time: 10 minutes

Servings: 4

Ingredients:

4 (4-ounce) fish fillets

Nonstick cooking spray

3 to 4 medium lemons

1 tablespoon extra-virgin olive oil

¼ teaspoon freshly ground black pepper

¼ teaspoon kosher or sea salt

Directions:

1. Using paper towels, pat the fillets dry and let stand at room temperature for 10 minutes.

2. Meanwhile, coat the cold cooking grate of the grill with nonstick cooking spray, and preheat the grill to 400°F or medium-high heat.

3. Slice one lemon in half and set half aside. Slice the remaining half of that lemon and the remaining lemons into ¼-inch-thick slices. (You should have about 12 to 16 lemon slices.)

4. Squeeze 1 tablespoon of juice out of the reserved lemon half into a small bowl.

5. Add the oil to the bowl with the lemon juice, and mix well. Put both sides of the fish with the oil mixture, and sprinkle evenly with pepper and salt.

6. Carefully place the lemon slices on the grill (or the grill pan), arranging 3 to 4 slices together in the shape of a fish fillet, and repeat with the remaining slices.

7. Place the fish fillets directly on the lemon slices and grill with the lid closed. (If you're grilling on the stove top, cover with a large pot lid or aluminum foil.)

8. Flip the fish halfway through the cooking time only if the fillets are more than half an inch thick.

9. It is cooked when it just starts to separate into flakes when pressed mildly with a fork.

Nutrition Calories 147 Fat 5g Carbs 1g Protein 22g

Weeknight Sheet Pan Fish Dinner

Preparation Time: 10 minutes

Cooking Time: 10 minutes

Servings: 4

Ingredients:

Nonstick cooking spray

2 tablespoons extra-virgin olive oil

1 tablespoon balsamic vinegar

4 (4-ounce) fish fillets (½ inch thick)

2½ cups green beans

1-pint cherry or grape tomatoes

Directions:

1. Preheat the oven to 400°F. Brush two large, rimmed baking sheets with nonstick cooking spray. In a small bowl, combine the oil and vinegar.

Set aside. Place two pieces of fish on each baking sheet.

2. In a large bowl, combine the beans and tomatoes. Pour in the oil and vinegar, and toss gently to coat.

3. Pour half of the green bean mixture over the fish on one baking sheet and the remaining half on the fish.

4. Turn the fish over, and rub it in the oil mixture to coat. Lay the vegetables evenly on the baking sheets so hot air can circulate them.

5. Bake until the fish is just opaque. It is cooked when it just begins to separate into chunks when pricked gently with a fork.

Nutrition Calories 193 Fat 8g Carbs 3g Protein 23g

Crispy Polenta Fish Sticks

Preparation Time: 10 minutes

Cooking Time: 15 minutes

Servings: 4

Ingredients:

2 large eggs, lightly beaten

1 tablespoon 2% milk

1-pound skinned fish fillets sliced into 20 (1-inch-wide) strips ½ cup yellow cornmeal

½ cup whole-wheat panko bread crumbs

¼ teaspoon smoked paprika

¼ teaspoon kosher or sea salt

¼ teaspoon freshly ground black pepper

Nonstick cooking spray

Directions:

1. Situate a large, rimmed baking sheet in the oven. Preheat the oven to 400°F with the pan inside.

2. In a large bowl, combine the eggs and milk. Then, using a fork, add the fish strips to the egg mixture and stir gently to coat.

3. Put the cornmeal, bread crumbs, smoked paprika, salt, and pepper in a quart-size zip-top plastic bag.

4. Using a fork or tongs, transfer the fish to the bag, letting the excess egg wash drip off into the bowl before transferring.

5. Seal tight and shake gently to coat each fish stick completely.

6. With oven mitts, carefully remove the hot baking sheet and spray it with nonstick cooking spray.

7. Using a fork or tongs, remove the fish sticks from the bag and arrange them on the hot baking sheet, with space between them so the hot air can circulate and crisp them up.

8. Bake for 5 to 8 minutes, until gentle pressure with a fork causes the fish to flake, and serve.

Nutrition Calories 256 Fat 6g Carbs 2g Protein 29g

Salmon Skillet Supper

Preparation Time: 15 minutes

Cooking Time: 15 minutes

Servings: 4

Ingredients:

1 tablespoon extra-virgin olive oil

2 garlic cloves minced

1 teaspoon smoked paprika

1-pint grape or cherry tomatoes, quartered

1 (12-ounce) jar of roasted red peppers

1 tablespoon water

¼ teaspoon freshly ground black pepper

¼ teaspoon kosher or sea salt

1-pound salmon fillets, skin removed, cut into 8 pieces 1 tablespoon freshly squeezed lemon juice (from ½ medium lemon)

Directions:

1. Over medium heat, cook the oil in a skillet. Mix in the garlic and smoked paprika and cook for 1 minute, stirring often.

2. Stir in the tomatoes, roasted peppers, water, black pepper, and salt.

3. Adjust the heat to medium-high, simmer, cook for 3 minutes and smash the tomatoes until the end of the cooking time.

4. Place the salmon in the skillet, and drizzle some of the sauce over the top.

5. Cover and cook for 10 to 12 minutes (145°F using a meat thermometer) and just start to flake.

6. Pull out the skillet from the heat, and sprinkle lemon juice over the top of the fish. Stir the sauce, then slice the salmon into chunks. Serve.

Nutrition Calories 289 Fat 13g Carbs 2g Protein 31g

Tuscan Tuna and Zucchini Burgers

Preparation Time: 10 minutes

Cooking Time: 30 minutes

Servings: 4

Ingredients:

3 slices of whole-wheat sandwich bread, toasted 2 (5-ounce) cans of tuna in olive oil

1 cup shredded zucchini

1 large egg, lightly beaten

¼ cup diced red bell pepper

1 tablespoon dried oregano

1 teaspoon lemon zest

¼ teaspoon freshly ground black pepper

¼ teaspoon kosher or sea salt

1 tablespoon extra-virgin olive oil

Salad greens or 4 whole-wheat rolls for serving (optional)
Directions:

1. Crumble the toast into bread crumbs using your fingers (or a knife to cut into ¼-inch cubes) until you have 1 cup of loosely packed crumbs.

2. Pour the crumbs into a large bowl. Add the tuna, zucchini, egg, bell pepper, oregano, lemon zest, black pepper, and salt.

3. Mix well with a fork.

4. Divide the mixture into four (½-cup-size) patties. Place on a plate, and press each patty flat to about ¾-inch thick.

5. Over medium-high heat, cook the oil in a skillet. Add the patties to the hot oil, then turn the heat down to medium.

6. Cook the patties for 5 minutes, flip with a spatula, and cook for an additional 5 minutes. Enjoy as-is or serve on salad greens or whole-wheat rolls.

Nutrition Calories 191 Fat 10g Carbs 2g Protein 15g

Sicilian Kale and Tuna Bowl
Preparation Time: 15 minutes

Cooking Time: 15 minutes

Servings: 6

Ingredients:

1-pound kale

3 tablespoons extra-virgin olive oil

1 cup chopped onion

3 garlic cloves, minced

1 (2.25-ounce) can of sliced olives, drained

¼ cup capers

¼ teaspoon red pepper

2 teaspoons sugar

2 (6-ounce) cans of tuna in olive oil

1 (15-ounce) can of cannellini beans

¼ teaspoon ground black pepper

¼ teaspoon kosher or sea salt

Directions:

1. Boil three-quarters full of water in a stock pot. Mix in the kale and cook for 2 minutes. Strain the kale with a colander and set it aside.

2. Return the empty pot to the stove over medium heat, and put in the oil.

3. Mix in the onion and cook for 4 minutes, continuous stirring. Place in the garlic and cook for 1 minute.

4. Place the olives, capers, and crushed red pepper, and cook for 1 minute.

5. Lastly, add the partially cooked kale and sugar, and stir until the kale is completely coated with oil. Close pot and cook for 8 minutes.

6. Pull out the kale from the heat, add the tuna, beans, pepper, and salt, and serve.

Nutrition Calories 265 Fat 12g Carbs 7g Protein 16g

Mediterranean Cod Stew

Preparation Time: 10 minutes

Cooking Time: 20 minutes

Servings: 6

Ingredients:

2 tablespoons extra-virgin olive oil

2 cups chopped onion

2 garlic cloves, minced

¾ teaspoon smoked paprika

1 (14.5-ounce) can of diced tomatoes, undrained 1 (12-ounce) jar of roasted red peppers

1 cup sliced olives, green or black

1/3 cup dry red wine

¼ teaspoon freshly ground black pepper

¼ teaspoon kosher or sea salt

1½ pounds cod fillets, cut into 1-inch pieces

3 cups sliced mushrooms

Directions:

1. Cook the oil in a stockpot. Mix in the onion and cook for 4 minutes, stirring occasionally. Stir in the garlic and smoked paprika and cook for 1 minute, stirring often.

2. Mix the tomatoes with their juices, roasted peppers, olives, wine, pepper, and salt, and turn the heat up to medium-high. Bring to a boil.

Add the cod and mushrooms, and reduce the heat to medium.

3. Cook for about 10 minutes, occasionally stirring, until the cod is cooked through and flakes easily, and serve.

Nutrition Calories 220 Fat 8g Carbs 3g Protein 28g

Rosemary Cod

Preparation Time: 10 minutes

Cooking Time: 3 hours

Servings: 2

Ingredients:

1 tablespoon olive oil

1-pound cod fillets, boneless

1 teaspoon sweet paprika

¼ cup chicken stock

2 scallions, chopped

½ teaspoon rosemary, dried

Directions:

1. In your slow cooker, mix the cod with the paprika, oil, and the other ingredients, toss gently, put the lid on, and cook on High for 3 hours.

2. Divide everything between plates and serve.

Nutrition: 252 calories,41g protein, 2g carbohydrates, 9.3g fat, 0.9g fiber, 111mg cholesterol, 240mg sodium, 71mg potassium.

Chili Tuna

Preparation Time: 10 minutes

Cooking Time: 2 hours

Servings: 6

Ingredients:

1-pound tuna fillets, boneless and cubed ½ teaspoon red pepper flakes, crushed ¼ teaspoon cayenne pepper

½ cup chicken stock

½ teaspoon chili powder

1 tablespoon olive oil

1 tablespoon chives, chopped

Directions:

1. In your slow cooker, mix the tuna with the pepper flakes, cayenne, and the other ingredients, toss, put the lid on and cook on High for 2 hours.

2. Divide the tuna mix between plates and serve.

Nutrition: 297 calories,16g protein, 0.3g carbohydrates, 25.9g fat, 0.1g fiber, 0mg cholesterol, 66mg sodium, 10mg potassium.

Lemon pepper salmon

Serves: 4

Planning: Time: quarter-hour

Ingredients:

4 salmon filets

Blended branches of dill, basil, tarragon and parsley 4 cuts lemon

1 zucchini, dig strips

1 carrot, dig strips

Preparation:

1. Add 1 cup of water to the Instant Pot. Add the branches of spices within the water.

2. Place the liner container inside. Put the salmon on top of the container.

3. Drizzle with a tablespoon of vegetable oil. Season with salt and pepper.

4. Top with lemon cuts. Cover the pot and set it to steam and cook for 3 minutes

5. Release the pressing factor rapidly. Move the fish to a spot and eliminate the lemon cuts.

6. Sauté the vegetables within the Instant pot for 2minutes.

7. Serve the salmon with the veggies.

Serving Suggestion: Garnish with new lemon wedges.

Dietary Information Per Serving:

Calories 252, Total Fat 11.1g, Saturated Fat 1.6g, Cholesterol 78mg, Sodium 94mg, Total Carbohydrate 3.8g, Dietary Fibre 1.1g, Total Sugars 1.8g, Protein 35.3g, Potassium 870mg

Shrimp in wine

Serves: 6

Arrangement: Time: quarter-hour

Ingredients:

1 tablespoon spread

1 tablespoon garlic, minced

2 lb. shrimp, stripped and deveined

1/2 cup chicken broth

1/2 cup wine

Preparation:

1. Set the moment Pot to sauté. Add the spread and, therefore, the garlic, cook for 30 seconds.

2. Pour within the stock and wine to deglaze.

3. Add the shrimp. Season with salt and pepper.

4. Cover the pot. Set it to manual and cook at a high pressing factor for 1 moment.

5. Release the pressing factor normally.

Serving Suggestion: Serve with rice or pasta.

Tips: you'll prepare with dried spices.

Nourishing Information Per Serving:

Calories 216, Total Fat 4.5g, Saturated Fat 2g, Cholesterol 324mg, Sodium 447mg, Total Carbohydrate 3.4g, Dietary Fibre 0g, Total Sugars 0.2g, Protein 34.6g, Potassium 283mg

Fish with Meuniere butter Sauce

Serves: 4

Readiness: Time: quarter-hour

Ingredients:

4 fish filets

1/4 cup juice

1 tablespoon new dill

1 tablespoon spread

Preparation:

1. Pour 1 cup water and juice within the Instant Pot.

2. Add the liner bin. Put the fillet on top of the bushel. Season with salt and pepper and dill.

3. Seal the pot. Pick a manual setting and cook at a high pressing factor for five minutes.

4. Release the pressing factor rapidly and eliminate the highest from the pot.

5. Place the margarine on top. Allow it to liquefy and afterwards serve.

Serving Suggestion: Serve with green beans.

Tips: Use newly crushed juice.

Nourishing Information Per Serving:

Calories 213, Total Fat 18.5g, Saturated Fat 1.9g, Cholesterol 8mg, Sodium 25mg, Total Carbohydrate 0.8g, Dietary Fibre 0.2g, Total Sugars 0.3g, Protein 10.8g, Potassium 46mg

Mediterranean cod

Serves: 6

Readiness: Time: 20 minutes

Ingredients:

6 cod fillets

1 onion, cut

1 tablespoon juice

1 teaspoon oregano

28 oz. canned diced tomatoes

Preparation:

1. Season the cod with salt and pepper.

2. Add 2 tablespoons of vegetable oil into the moment Pot.

3. Set it to sauté. Add the cod and cook for 3 minutes for each side.

4. Add the rest of the ingredients. Blend well.

5. Cover the pot. Pick manual capacity and cook at high pressing factor for five minutes.

6. Release the pressing factor rapidly. Pour the sauce over the cod before serving.

Serving Suggestion: Serve with soup or plate of mixed greens.

Tip: you'll likewise utilize other white fish filets for this formula.

Nourishing Information Per Serving:

Calories 123, Total Fat 1.3g, Saturated Fat 0.1g, Cholesterol 55mg, Sodium 78mg, Total Carbohydrate 7.1g, Dietary Fibre 2.1g, Total Sugars 4.3g, Protein 21.4g, Potassium 348mg

Shrimp with Tomatoes and Feta

Serves: 4

Readiness: Time: 20 minutes

Ingredients:

2 tablespoons margarine

1 tablespoon garlic, minced

1 lb. shrimp, stripped and deveined

14 oz. canned squashed tomatoes

1 cup feta cheddar, disintegrated

Preparation:

1. Set the moment Pot to sauté. Add the margarine and stay for it to dissolve.

2. Add the garlic and cook until fragrant.

3. Add the shrimp and tomatoes.

4. Seal the pot. Set it to manual and cook at low pressing factor for 1 moment.

5. Release the pressing factor rapidly. Top with the feta cheddar.

Serving Suggestion: Serve with entire wheat toasted bread.

Tip: you'll likewise pack up with olives.

Wholesome Information Per Serving:

Calories 218, Total Fat 10.5g, Saturated Fat 6.6g, Cholesterol 192mg, Sodium 618mg, Total Carbohydrate 7.9g, Dietary Fibre 2.2g, Total Sugars 4.7g, Protein 22.5g, Potassium 150mg

Mussels in spread Sauce

Serves: 4

Planning: Time: 20 minutes

Ingredients:

2 tablespoons margarine

4 cloves garlic, minced

1/2 cup stock

1/2 cup wine

2 lb. mussels, cleaned and facial hair eliminated

Preparation: 1. Add the spread and garlic within the Instant Pot.

2. Switch it to sauté. Cook until fragrant.

3. Pour within the stock and wine. Add the mussels.

4. Cover the pot. Set it to manual and cook at a high pressing factor for five minutes.

5. Release the pressing factor rapidly.

Serving Suggestion: Sprinkle hacked parsley on top.

Tips: Discard opened mussels before Cooking and people that did not open after cooking.

Healthful Information Per Serving: Calories 280, Total Fat 11g, Saturated Fat 4.7g, Cholesterol 79mg, Sodium 787mg, Total Carbohydrate 10.3g, Dietary Fibre 0.1g, Total Sugars 0.4g, Protein 27.9g, Potassium 795mg

Fish Stew with Tomatoes and Olives

Serves: 4

Arrangement: Time: quarter-hour

Ingredients:

1/2 lb. halibut filet

4 cloves garlic, minced

1 cup cherry tomatoes, hamper the centre

3 cups tomato soup

1 cup green olives, hollowed and cut

Preparation:

1. Season the fish with salt and pepper.

2. Pour 1 tablespoon vegetable oil into the moment Pot. Add the garlic and cook until fragrant.

3. Add the fish and cook for 3 minutes for every side.

4. Add the rest of the ingredients.

5. Cover the pot. Select manual capacity and cook at low pressing factor for 3 minutes.

6. Release the pressing factor rapidly.

Serving Suggestion: Drizzle with vegetable oil and sprinkle with hacked new cilantro.

Tip: you'll likewise sprinkle spices on the 2 sides of the fillet.

Healthful Information Per Serving:

Calories 245, Total Fat 3.7g, Saturated Fat 0.6g, Cholesterol 35mg, Sodium 1098mg, Total Carbohydrate 28g, Dietary Fibre 2.9g, Total Sugars 16.5g, Protein 26.3g, Potassium 1040mg

Rosemary salmon

Serves: 3

Readiness: Time: 20 minutes

Ingredients:

1 lb. salmon filets

10 oz. new asparagus

1 twig new rosemary

1/2 cup cherry tomatoes, dig equal parts

Dressing (a combination of 1 tablespoon vegetable oil and 1 tablespoon juice)

Preparation:

1. Add 1 cup of water into the moment Pot. Spot the liner rack inside.

2. Put the salmon fillets on the rack. Add the rosemary and asparagus on top of the salmon.

3. Cover the pot. Select manual setting and cook at high pressing factor for 3 minutes.

4. Release the pressing factor rapidly.

5. Transfer to a plate. Spot the tomatoes as an afterthought.

6. Drizzle with the dressing.

Serving Suggestion: Garnish with lemon cuts.

Dietary Information Per Serving:

Calories 267, Total Fat 14.3g, Saturated Fat 2.1g, Cholesterol 67mg, Sodium 71mg, Total Carbohydrate 5.2g, Dietary Fibre 2.5g, Total Sugars 2.7g, Protein 31.7g, Potassium 853mg

Salmon with Tahini Sauce
Serves: 2

Arrangement: Time: 10 minutes **Ingredients:**

1 lb. salmon filets

3 tablespoons tahini sauce

2 lemon cuts

2 twigs new rosemary

Preparation:

1. Add the water to the moment Pot.

2. Place a liner bushel inside. Put the salmon on top of the container.

3. Season with salt and pepper. Spot rosemary and lemon cut on top.

4. Cover the pot. Set it to manual and cook at a high pressing factor for 3 minutes.

5. Release the pressing factor rapidly.

6. Drizzle the tahini sauce on top before serving.

Serving Suggestion: Garnish with new lemon wedges.

Tips: If you cannot discover tahini sauce, you'll make your own by blending the accompanying: 1 tablespoon wine vinegar, 1 tablespoon lemon juice, 1 clove garlic, minced, ¼ teaspoon dried oregano, Salt and pepper to taste, ¼ cup vegetable oil, 1 tablespoon disintegrated feta cheddar.

Nourishing Information Per Serving:

Calories 306, Total Fat 14.2g, Saturated Fat 2.1g, Cholesterol 100mg, Sodium 101mg, Total Carbohydrate 1.4g, Dietary Fibre 0.7g, Total Sugars 0.2g, Protein 44.1g, Potassium 892mg

Fish and Potatoes

Serves: 4

Readiness: Time: quarter-hour

Ingredients:

1 lb. cod filets, dig strips.

1 onion, hacked

1 lb. potatoes, dig 3D squares

4 cups vegetable stock

1 teaspoon old inlet preparing

Preparation:

1. Season the salmon filets with salt and pepper.

2. Pour 1 tablespoon vegetable oil within the Instant Pot.

3. Add the onion and cook for 3 minutes.

4. Add the salmon and cook for 1 moment for each side.

5. Pour within the stock and add the potatoes, and preparing.

6. Seal the pot. Go it to manual and cook at high pressing factor for 3 minutes.

7. Release the pressing factor rapidly.

Serving Suggestion: Top with slashed new parsley.

Wholesome Information Per Serving:

Calories 278, Total Fat 8.5g, Saturated Fat 1.4g, Cholesterol 50mg, Sodium 981mg, Total Carbohydrate 21.3g, Dietary Fibre 3.3g, Total Sugars 3.2g, Protein 29.1g, Potassium 1144mg

Mediterranean Baked Fish Recipe with Tomatoes and Capers

Preparation Time: 15 minutes

Cooking Time: 20 minutes

Servings: 1

Ingredients:

⅓ cup extra virgin olive oil

One small red onion, finely chopped

Two large tomatoes diced (3 cups diced tomatoes. Use quality canned tomatoes if you like)

Ten garlic cloves, chopped

1 ½ tsp organic ground coriander

1 tsp all-natural sweet Spanish paprika

1 tsp organic ground cumin

½ tsp cayenne pepper (optional)

1 ½ tbsp capers

Fresh parsley or mint for garnish

Salt and pepper

⅓ cup golden raisins

1 ½ lb. white fish fillet

Juice of ½ lemon or more to your liking

Zest of 1 lemon

Directions:

Ø Make the sauce with the tomatoes and capers. Heat extra virgin olive oil in a medium saucepan over medium-high heat until shimmering but not smoking. Cook for 3 minutes, often stirring, until the onions begin to turn gold in color. Toss in the tomatoes, garlic, spices, a bit of salt and pepper (not too much), capers, and raisins. Bring to a boil, then reduce to medium-low heat and leave to simmer for about 15 minutes.

Ø Preheat the oven to 400°F.

Ø Pat the fish dry and season both sides with salt and pepper.

Ø Twelve cooked tomato sauces should be poured into the bottom of a 9 12" x 13" baking dish. Place the fish on top. Top with the leftover tomato sauce after adding the lemon juice and zest.

Ø Bake at 400°F for 15 to 18 minutes, or until the fish is cooked through and flakes readily (do not over-cook). If desired, remove from the heat and garnish with fresh parsley or mint.

Ø Serve hot with grilled zucchini from the Mediterranean, Greek potatoes, or Lebanese rice. (Also, see the page for other side choices or salads.)

Grilled Swordfish Recipe with a Mediterranean Twist

Preparation Time: 15 minutes

Cooking Time: 20 minutes

Servings: 1

Ingredients:

½ to 1 teaspoon sweet Spanish paprika

¾ tsp salt

½ tsp freshly ground black pepper

Four swordfish steaks, about 5 to 6 ounces each, from sustainable sources

⅓ cup extra virgin olive oil

Crushed red pepper, optional

1 tsp coriander

6 to 12 garlic cloves, peeled

2 tbsp fresh lemon juice

¾ tsp cumin

Directions:

Ø Blend the garlic, lemon juice, olive oil, spices, salt, and pepper in a food processor for about three minutes, or until well blended, making a thick and smooth marinade.

Ø Pat the swordfish steaks dry, place them in a pan (or a dish with sides), and generously apply the marinade to both sides. Set aside for 15 minutes or so while the grill heats up.

Ø Preheat a gas grill to high heat (be sure to oil the grates before using). When ready, grill the fish steaks over high heat for 5 to 6 minutes on one side, then turn over and cook for another 3 minutes or so on the other side. There will certainly be some pink on the inside, but it should be cooked through when it reaches the table).

Ø Finish with a splash of fresh lemon juice and, if desired, a sprinkling of crushed red pepper flakes. Enjoy!

Sicilian-Style Fish Stew Recipe

Preparation Time: 15 minutes

Cooking Time: 20 minutes

Servings: 1

Ingredients:

Private Reserve extra virgin olive oil

One large yellow onion, chopped

Two celery ribs, chopped

1 28-oz can whole peeled plum tomatoes

¼ cup golden raisins

3 cups low-sodium vegetable broth

2 tbsp capers, rinsed

2 lb. skinless sea bass fillet, about one ½-inch thick ½ cup chopped fresh parsley leaves stems removed 3 tbsp toasted pine nuts, optional

Crusty Italian bread for serving

Salt and pepper

Four large garlic cloves, minced

½ tsp dried thyme

Pinch red pepper flakes

¾ cup dry white wine

Directions:

Ø Heat one tablespoon olive oil over medium heat in a 5-quart Dutch oven (like this one). Add the onions, celery, and a pinch of salt and pepper (12 tsp each). Cook, often stirring, until the vegetables are softened (about 4 minutes). Cook for a few minutes until the thyme, red pepper flakes, and garlic are aromatic (about 30 more seconds).

Ø Stir in the white wine and tomato juice from the can. Bring to a simmer and boil until the liquid has been reduced by about 12 percent. Combine the tomatoes, vegetable broth, raisins, and capers in a mixing bowl. Cook for 15-20 minutes over medium heat or until the flavors meld.

Ø Pat the fish dry and season with salt and pepper to taste. Place the fish pieces in the cooking liquid and gently swirl everything together so that the fish pieces are well coated in the cooking liquid. Bring to a simmer and continue to boil for 5 minutes. Turn off the heat and cover the Dutch oven. Allow to rest off the heat for another 4-5 minutes to allow the fish to finish frying. It should be flaky when carefully pulling apart the fish with a paring knife. Finally, add the chopped parsley.

Ø If desired, spoon the hot fish stew into serving dishes and garnish with toasted pine nuts. Serve with crusty bread of your choice! Enjoy!

VEGETABLE RECIPES

Balsamic Brussels sprouts

Preparation Time: 10 minutes

Cooking Time: 4 hours and 10 minutes

Servings: 6

Ingredients:

2 tablespoons brown sugar

½ cup balsamic vinegar

2 lb. Brussels sprouts, trimmed and sliced in half 2 tablespoons olive oil 2 tablespoons butter, cut into cubes

Salt and pepper to taste

¼ cup Parmesan cheese, grated

Directions:

1. Put the brown sugar and vinegar in a saucepan over medium heat.

1. Mix and bring to a boil. Reduce heat and simmer for 8 minutes. Let cool and set aside.

2. Mix the Brussel sprouts in olive oil plus butter. Season with salt and pepper. Cover the pot. Cook low for 4 hours. Drizzle the balsamic vinegar on top of the Brussels sprouts. Sprinkle the Parmesan cheese on top.

Nutrition: Calories 193 Fat 10 g Cholesterol 13.2 mg Carbohydrate 21.9 g Fiber 6.2 g Protein 6.9 g Sugars 11.1 g

Mediterranean Zucchini & Eggplant

Preparation Time: 15 minutes

Cooking Time: 3 hours

Servings: 4

Ingredients:

1 tablespoon olive oil

1 onion, diced

4 cloves garlic, minced

1 red bell pepper, chopped

4 tomatoes, diced

1 zucchini, chopped

1 lb. eggplant, sliced into cubes

Salt and pepper to taste

2 teaspoons dried basil

4 oz. feta cheese

Directions:

1. Coat your slow cooker with olive oil. Mix all the fixing except cheese in the pot. Cook on high within 3 hours. Sprinkle feta cheese on top and serve.

Nutrition: Calories 341 Fat 12 g Cholesterol 25 mg Carbohydrate 51 g Fiber 11 g Protein 13 g Sugars 13 g

Roasted Baby Carrots

Preparation Time: 15 minutes

Cooking Time: 6 hours

Servings: 6

Ingredients:

2 lb. baby carrots

¼ cup apricot preserve

6 tablespoons butter

2 tablespoons honey

1 tablespoon sugar

1 teaspoon balsamic vinegar

1 teaspoon garlic powder

Salt and pepper to taste

¼ teaspoon dried thyme

¼ teaspoon ground mustard

Directions:

1. Combine all the fixing in the slow cooker. Mix well. Cover the pot.

2. Cook on low for 6 hours.

Nutrition: Calories 218 Fat 11.8g Cholesterol 31mg Sodium 206mg Carbohydrate 29.3g Fiber 4.5g Sugars 20.9g Protein 1.3g

Artichokes with Garlic & Cream Sauce

Preparation Time: 15 minutes

Cooking Time: 8 hours

Servings: 6

Ingredients:

Cooking spray

30 oz. canned diced tomatoes

6 cloves garlic, crushed and minced

28 oz. canned artichoke hearts, rinsed, drained, and sliced into quarters ½ cup whipping cream

1 teaspoon dried basil

½ teaspoon dried oregano

Feta cheese

Directions:

1. Spray the slow cooker with oil. Add the tomatoes with juice, garlic, and artichoke hearts. Season with basil and oregano. Mix well.

2. Cover the pot. Cook on low for 8 hours. Stir in the cream. Let's sit for 5 minutes. Top with the crumbled cheese.

Nutrition: Calories 403 Fat 5 g Cholesterol 27 mg Carbohydrate 38 g Fiber 5 g Protein 13 g Sugars 17 g

Mediterranean Kale & White Kidney Beans

Preparation Time: 30 minutes

Cooking Time: 3 hours

Servings: 6

Ingredients:

1 onion, chopped

4 cloves garlic, crushed

¼ cup celery, chopped

2 carrots, sliced

1 cup farro, rinsed and drained

14 oz. canned roasted tomatoes

4 cups low-sodium vegetable broth

½ teaspoon red pepper, crushed

Salt to taste

3 tablespoons freshly squeezed lemon juice

15-ounce white kidney beans, drained

4 cup kale

½ cup feta cheese, crumbled

Fresh parsley, chopped

Directions:

1. Put the onion, garlic, celery, carrots, farro, tomatoes, broth, red pepper, and salt in your slow cooker. Seal the pot. Cook on high for 2 hours. Stir in the lemon juice, beans, and kale. Cover and

cook for 1 more hour. Sprinkle the cheese and parsley before serving.

Nutrition: Calories 274 Fat 9 g Cholesterol 11 mg Carbohydrate 46 g Fiber 9 g Protein 14 g Sugars 6 g

Creamed Corn

Preparation Time: 10 minutes

Cooking Time: 4 hours

Servings: 12

Ingredients:

16 oz. frozen corn kernels

8 oz. cream cheese

½ cup butter

½ cup milk

1 tablespoon white sugar

Salt and pepper to taste

Directions:

1. Put all the listed fixing in the slow cooker. Stir well. Cook on high for 4 hours.

Nutrition: Calories 192 Fat 15 g Cholesterol 42 mg Carbohydrate 13.7 g Fiber 1.3 g Protein 3.4 g Sugars 3 g

Spicy Beans & Veggies

Preparation Time: 20 minutes

Cooking Time: 8 hours

Servings: 6

Ingredients:

15 ounces canned northern beans, drained

15 oz. canned red beans, rinsed and drained

5 teaspoons garlic, minced

1 onion, chopped

1 cup, sliced thinly

½ cup celery, sliced thinly

2 cups green beans, trimmed and sliced

2 red chili peppers, chopped

2 bay leaves

Salt and pepper to taste

Directions:

1. Mix all the fixing listed above in the slow cooker. Set it on low.

2. Seal and cook for 8 hours. Discard the bay leaves before serving.

Nutrition: Calories 264 Fat 0.9g Carbohydrate 49g Sugars 3g Protein 17.2g Potassium 1111mg

Eggplant Salad

Preparation Time: 10 minutes

Cooking Time: 8 hours

Servings: 4

Ingredients:

1 onion, sliced

1 green bell pepper, sliced

1 red bell pepper, sliced

24 oz. canned tomatoes

1 eggplant, sliced

2 teaspoons cumin

1 tablespoon smoked paprika

1 tablespoon lemon juice

Salt and pepper to taste

Directions:

1. Add all the fixings to the slow cooker. Mix well. Cook on low within 8 hours.

Nutrition: Calories 90 Fat 1.1g Sodium 16mg Carbohydrate 19.7g Fiber 7.9g Sugars 10.9g Protein 3.7g Potassium 826mg

Turkish Stuffed Eggplant

Preparation Time: 15 minutes

Cooking Time: 4 hours

Servings: 6

Ingredients:

½ cup extra-virgin olive oil

3 small eggplants

1 teaspoon of sea salt

½ teaspoon black pepper

1 large yellow onion, finely chopped

4 garlic cloves, minced

one 15-ounce can dice tomatoes, with the juice

¼ cup finely chopped fresh flat-leaf parsley

six 8-inch round pita bread, quartered and toasted 1 cup plain Greek-style yogurt

Directions:

1. Pour ¼ cup of olive oil into the slow cooker and generously coat the interior of the crock. Cut each eggplant in half lengthwise.

2. You can leave the stem on. Score the cut side of each half every ¼ inch.

3. Arrange the eggplant halves, skin-side down, in the slow cooker.

4. Sprinkle with 1 teaspoon salt and ½ teaspoon pepper. In a large skillet, heat the remaining ¼ cup of olive oil over medium-high heat.

5. Sauté the onion and garlic for 3 minutes, or until the onion softens. Add the tomatoes and parsley to the skillet. Season with salt and pepper. Sauté for another 5 minutes until the liquid has almost evaporated. Using a large spoon, spoon the tomato mixture over the eggplants, covering each half with some mixtures. Cover and cook on high within 2 hours or low for 4 hours.

6. Uncover the slow cooker, and let the eggplant rest for 10 minutes.

7. Then transfer the eggplant to a serving dish. If there is any juice in the bottom of the cooker, spoon it over the eggplant. Serve hot with toasted pita wedges and yogurt on the side.

Nutrition: Calories: 56 Carbs: 10g Fat: 2g Protein: 2g

Eggplant Parmigiana

Preparation Time: 15 minutes

Cooking Time: 5 hours

Servings: 6

Ingredients:

4 mediums to large eggplants, peeled sea salt for sweating eggplants, plus 1 teaspoon 2 eggs, lightly beaten

1/3 cup vegetable stock

3 tablespoons all-purpose flour

olive oil for frying (about ½ cup)

1/3 cup seasoned bread crumbs

½ cup grated parmesan cheese, preferably Parmigiano-Reggiano, 1

tablespoon extra-virgin olive oil

1 yellow onion, chopped

1 28-ounce can crush tomatoes, with the juice

1 6-ounce can of tomato paste

4 tablespoons chopped fresh parsley

2 cloves garlic, minced

1 teaspoon dried oregano

1 teaspoon of sea salt

¼ teaspoon black pepper

½ cup white wine

16 ounces mozzarella cheese, sliced

Directions:

1. To prepare the eggplant, first, sweat it. Next, cut the eggplant into ½- inch slices. Put in a large bowl in layers, flavoring each layer with salt. Let it set within 30 minutes to drain excess moisture.

2. Mix the eggs with the stock and flour until smooth in a shallow bowl. Soak the eggplant slices in the batter.

3. Warm up 1 tablespoon of the olive oil for frying in a skillet. Sauté the eggplant in hot olive oil within. Put aside the eggplant on a paper towel-lined plate. Mix the seasoned bread crumbs with the Parmesan cheese in a small bowl. Set aside.

4. Warm-up extra-virgin olive oil in a large skillet over medium heat.

5. Put the onion, then sauté within 3 minutes until the onion softens. Add the crushed tomatoes, tomato paste, parsley, garlic, oregano, 1 teaspoon sea salt, ¼ teaspoon black pepper, and the white wine.

6. Put the fixing in even layers in your slow cooker, in this order: ¼ of the eggplant slices, 1/4 of the bread crumbs, 1/4 of the tomato mixture, and 1/4 of the mozzarella cheese.

7. Repeat the process by making three more layers of the eggplant, bread crumbs, tomato mixture, and mozzarella. Cover and cook on low within 4 to 5 hours. Serve hot.

Nutrition: Calories: 270 Carbs: 26g Fat: 15g Protein: 8g

Garlic-butter Asparagus With Parmesan

Servings:2

Cooking Time: 8 Minutes

Ingredients:

1 cup water

1 pound asparagus, trimmed

2 cloves garlic, chopped

3 tablespoons almond butter

Salt and ground black pepper, to taste

3 tablespoons grated Parmesan cheese

Directions:

1. Pour the water into the Instant Pot and insert a trivet.

2. Put the asparagus on a tin foil add the butter and garlic. Season to taste with salt and pepper.

3. Fold over the foil and seal the asparagus inside so the foil doesn't come open. Arrange the asparagus on the trivet.

4. Secure the lid. Select the Manual mode and set the cooking time for 8 minutes at High Pressure.

5. Once cooking is complete, do a quick pressure release. Carefully open the lid.

6. Unwrap the foil packet and serve sprinkled with the Parmesan cheese.

Nutrition Info: Per Serving: Calories: 243;Fat: 15.7g;Protein: 12.3g;Carbs: 15.3g.

Baked Veggie Medley

Servings:4

Cooking Time:70 Minutes

Ingredients:

2 tbsp olive oil

½ lb green beans, trimmed

1 tomato, chopped

1 potato, sliced

½ tbsp tomato paste

2 tbsp chopped fresh parsley

1 tsp sweet paprika

1 onion, sliced

1 cup mushrooms, sliced

1 celery stalk, chopped

1 red bell pepper, sliced

1 eggplant, sliced

½ cup vegetable broth

Salt and black pepper to taste

Directions:

1. Preheat oven to 375°F. Warm oil in a skillet over medium heat and sauté onion, bell pepper, celery, and mushrooms for 5 minutes until tender. Stir in paprika and tomato paste for 1 minute. Pour in the vegetable broth and stir. Combine the remaining ingredients in a baking pan and mix in the sautéed vegetable. Bake covered with foil for 40-50 minutes.

Nutrition Info: Per Serving: Calories: 175;Fat: 8g;Protein: 5.2g;Carbs: 25.2g.

Baked Honey Acorn Squash

Servings:4

Cooking Time:35 Minutes

Ingredients:

1 acorn squash, cut into wedges

2 tbsp olive oil

2 tbsp honey

2 tbsp rosemary, chopped

2 tbsp walnuts, chopped

Directions:

1. Preheat oven to 400°F. In a bowl, mix honey, rosemary, and olive oil. Lay the squash wedges on a baking sheet and drizzle with the honey mixture. Bake for 30 minutes until squash is tender and slightly caramelized, turning each slice over halfway through. Serve cooled sprinkled with walnuts.

Pea & Carrot Noodles

Servings:4

Cooking Time:25 Minutes

Ingredients:

2 tbsp olive oil

4 carrots, spiralized

1 sweet onion, chopped

2 cups peas

2 garlic cloves, minced

¼ cup chopped fresh parsley

Salt and black pepper to taste

Directions:

1. Warm 2 tbsp of olive oil in a pot over medium heat and sauté the onion and garlic for 3 minutes until just tender and fragrant. Add in spiralized carrots and cook for 4 minutes. Mix in peas, salt, and pepper and cook for 4 minutes. Drizzle with the remaining olive oil and sprinkle with parsley.

Nutrition Info:

Per Serving: Calories: 157;Fat: 7g;Protein: 4.8g;Carbs: 19.6g.

Vegetable And Tofu Scramble

Servings:2

Cooking Time: 10 Minutes

Ingredients:

2 tablespoons extra-virgin olive oil

½ red onion, finely chopped

1 cup chopped kale

8 ounces mushrooms, sliced

8 ounces tofu, cut into pieces

2 garlic cloves, minced

Pinch red pepper flakes

½ teaspoon sea salt

⅛ teaspoon freshly ground black pepper

Directions:

1. Heat the olive oil in a medium nonstick skillet over medium-high heat until shimmering.

2. Add the onion, kale, and mushrooms to the skillet and cook for about 5 minutes, stirring occasionally, or until the vegetables start to brown.

3. Add the tofu and stir-fry for 3 to 4 minutes until softened.

4. Stir in the garlic, red pepper flakes, salt, and black pepper and cook for 30 seconds.

5. Let the mixture cool for 5 minutes before serving.

Tahini & Feta Butternut Squash

Servings:6

Cooking Time:50 Minutes

Ingredients:

3 lb butternut squash, peeled, halved lengthwise, and seeded 3 tbsp olive oil

Salt and black pepper to taste

2 tbsp fresh thyme, chopped

1 tbsp tahini

1 ½ tsp lemon juice

1 tsp honey

1 oz feta cheese, crumbled

¼ cup pistachios, chopped

Directions:

1. Preheat oven to 425°F. Slice the squash halves crosswise into ½-inch-thick pieces. Toss them with 2 tablespoons of olive oil, salt, and pepper and arrange them on a greased baking sheet in an even layer. Roast for 45-50 minutes or until golden and tender. Transfer squash to a serving platter. Whisk tahini, lemon juice, honey, remaining oil, and salt together in a bowl. Drizzle squash with tahini dressing and sprinkle with feta, pistachios, and thyme. Serve and enjoy!

Nutrition Info: Per Serving: Calories: 212;Fat: 12g;Protein: 4.1g;Carbs: 27g.

Mini Crustless Spinach Quiches

Servings:6

Cooking Time: 20 Minutes

Ingredients:

2 tablespoons extra-virgin olive oil

1 onion, finely chopped

2 cups baby spinach

2 garlic cloves, minced

8 large eggs, beaten

¼ cup unsweetened almond milk

½ teaspoon sea salt

¼ teaspoon freshly ground black pepper

1 cup shredded Swiss cheese

Cooking spray

Directions:

1. Preheat the oven to 375ºF. Spritz a 6-cup muffin tin with cooking spray. Set aside.

2. In a large skillet over medium-high heat, heat the olive oil until shimmering. Add the onion and cook for about 4 minutes, or until soft. Add the spinach and cook for about 1 minute, stirring constantly, or until the spinach softens. Add the garlic and sauté for 30 seconds. Remove from the heat and let cool.

3. In a medium bowl, whisk together the eggs, milk, salt and pepper.

4. Stir the cooled vegetables and the cheese into the egg mixture. Spoon the mixture into the prepared muffin tins. Bake for about 15 minutes, or until the eggs are set.

5. Let rest for 5 minutes before serving.

Nutrition Info: Per Serving: Calories: 218;Fat: 17.0g;Protein: 14.0g;Carbs: 4.0g.

Beet And Watercress Salad

Servings:4

Cooking Time: 8 Minutes

Ingredients:

2 pounds beets, scrubbed, trimmed and cut into ¾-inch pieces ½ cup water

1 teaspoon caraway seeds

½ teaspoon table salt, plus more for seasoning 1 cup plain Greek yogurt

1 small garlic clove, minced

5 ounces watercress, torn into bite-size pieces 1 tablespoon extra-virgin olive oil, divided, plus more for drizzling 1 tablespoon white wine vinegar, divided

Black pepper, to taste

1 teaspoon grated orange zest

2 tablespoons orange juice

¼ cup coarsely chopped fresh dill

¼ cup hazelnuts, toasted, skinned and chopped Coarse sea salt, to taste

Directions:

1. Combine the beets, water, caraway seeds and table salt in the Instant Pot. Set the lid in place. Select the Manual mode and set the cooking time for 8 minutes on High Pressure. When the timer goes off, do a quick pressure release.

2. Carefully open the lid. Using a slotted spoon, transfer the beets to a plate. Set aside to cool slightly.

3. In a small bowl, combine the yogurt, garlic and 3 tablespoons of the beet cooking liquid. In a large bowl, toss the watercress with 2 teaspoons of the oil and 1 teaspoon of the vinegar. Season with table salt and pepper.

4. Spread the yogurt mixture over a serving dish. Arrange the watercress on top of the yogurt mixture, leaving 1-inch border of the yogurt mixture.

5. Add the beets to now-empty large bowl and toss with the orange zest and juice, the remaining 2 teaspoons of the vinegar and the remaining 1 teaspoon of the oil. Season with table salt and pepper.

6. Arrange the beets on top of the watercress mixture. Drizzle with the olive oil and sprinkle with the dill, hazelnuts and sea salt.

Nutrition Info:Per Serving: Calories: 240;Fat: 15.0g;Protein: 9.0g;Carbs: 19.0g.

Baked Tomatoes And Chickpeas

Servings:4

Cooking Time: 40 To 45 Minutes

Ingredients:

1 tablespoon extra-virgin olive oil
½ medium onion, chopped
3 garlic cloves, chopped
¼ teaspoon ground cumin
2 teaspoons smoked paprika
2 cans chickpeas, drained and rinsed
4 cups halved cherry tomatoes
½ cup plain Greek yogurt, for serving
1 cup crumbled feta cheese, for serving
Directions:

1. Preheat the oven to 425ºF.

2. Heat the olive oil in an ovenproof skillet over medium heat.

3. Add the onion and garlic and sauté for about 5 minutes, stirring occasionally, or until tender and fragrant.

4. Add the paprika and cumin and cook for 2 minutes. Stir in the chickpeas and tomatoes and allow to simmer for 5 to 10 minutes.

5. Transfer the skillet to the preheated oven and roast for 25 to 30

minutes, or until the mixture bubbles and thickens.

6. Remove from the oven and serve topped with yogurt and crumbled feta cheese.

Nutrition Info: Per Serving: Calories: 411;Fat: 14.9g;Protein: 20.2g;Carbs: 50.7g.